Personal and Business Accounting with QuickBooks

Simplified Using QuickBooks 2020 Desktop and Real-World Cases
New Edition

By

Fraidun Besharat

Copyright © 2020 Fraidun Besharat

ISBN- KDP: 9798653586675

All rights reserved. No part of this publication may be reproduced, scanned, transmitted, or distributed in any printed or electronic form or by any means, including photocopying, recording, or other electronic methods without written permission from the author or publisher, except for the use of brief quotations in a book review or other noncommercial use permitted by law. Please do not participate in or encourage piracy of copyrighted materials in violation of the author's rights.

Photographs used with permission. Any references to historical events, real people, and real company names are used fictitiously as "real-world examples" throughout this book.

Published by Amazon Kindle Direct Publishing in 2020

First Edition published in USA

Contact the author:

fraidunmba@gmail.com

www.fraidunbesharat.com

Table of Contents

Introduction vii
About The Author viii
Significant Things Covered In This Book ix

PART ONE

Learning Objectives (Fundamental Accounting) 2

THE BOOKKEEPING AND DOUBLE ENTRY 2

Defining accounting 2
Defining Bookkeeping 2
Accrual vs. Cash Basis of Accounting 3
The Accounts 3
The Accounting Equation 3
Defining Debit and Credit 5
    Some Everyday Use Of Debit And Credit: 5
Journal Entries 6
T-Accounts 7
Adjusting Entry 7
General Ledger 8
Summary of the Accounting Cycle 8
Petty Cash 9
Bank Reconciliation 9
Financial Statements 10
Recording Transactions in Balance Sheet 11
Accounts Receivable and Payable 13
Preparing an Income Statement 13
Depreciation 15
Preparing Cash Flow Statement 17
Relation of Depreciation and Financial Statements 17
Depreciation Methods 19

Bookkeeping 19

PART TWO

Real-World Example To Complete Accounting Cycle 23

GENERAL OVERVIEW ON QUICKBOOKS 40

Importance of Learning to Use QuickBooks 40
Versions of QuickBooks 41
New 2020 Features in QuickBooks 41
Difference between QuickBooks Desktop and QuickBooks Online 42
Setting Up and Creating a Company 42
Introduction: Homepage & Document Center 43
Setting Up Users with Different Access Permissions/Role/Password 45
Track Changes and User Entry in QB (Audit Log/Trail) 49
Creating a Standard Chart of Accounts, Printing, and Sharing 50
    Here is how creating new accounts works: 52
Backing Up QuickBooks Files Automatically and Regularly 52
Opening and Restoring Existing Company Files 54
    How to Restore a File or Open a Previous Backup File: 54
Switching to Single-User Mode and Multi-Users Networking 55
Importing and Exporting QuickBooks Data with MS Excel Files 56
Closing the Book and Securing 57
Adding Priority to Do List and Reminders 59
Managing Currencies, Setting Up Home Currency vs. Multiple Currencies
    Turning on Multicurrency and Setting Up Home Currency 60
Enter and Track Vehicle Mileage 61
Preparing Letters with Envelopes 62
    Use the following steps to prepare envelopes: 62
Adding items/categories of products/services list 64
Class List and Business Units/Locations/Projects 66

How to Activate a Class List 66

Adding Pricing Lists 71

Managing Sales Tax and Calculation 72
How to Record Sales Tax in QuickBooks 72

Discount Item List 73

Setting Up Your Employee List and Other Details 74

Vendor/Supplier Setup and Tracking Payables/Purchases onCredit 77

SettingUp Vendors (if 1099 Applies forYear-End Purposes) 78

Creating a Purchase Order (PO), EnteringBills, PayingBills 78
Creating a purchase order (PO): 78

EnteringBills for Payment and Reimbursement 79
How to enter a bill: 79

Inventory Management 79
Create New Item, Adjust the Quantity, and Value in the Stock 79

Check physical inventory in stock 81

Inventory Assembly 81

ManagingSales Tax 83

Creating And Setting Up Customers 84

Creating New Customer Account 84

CreatingEstimatesor Quotations 85

CreatingSales Orders 85
Creating sales orders from an estimate: 87

CreatingInvoicesand Sales Receipt (Selling on Cash/Credit) 88

CreatingStatements and AssessingFinanceCharges 89

ReceivingPaymentsvia Cash, Check, Debit or E-Check Against Invoice 92

Recording Refunds and Credits Refundedto Customer 93

Automatic Invoice Entry "Memories" 93

AddingJobs and Applying Multiple Projects 94

Customizing Your Invoice and Other Forms 95

Adding Logos and Customizing Invoices 96

Banking and Reconciliation 99

Making Journal Entries: Double Entry Bookkeeping 100
Finding & SearchingTransactions and Other Information Faster (Invoice, Bill, PO) 101

Reporting In QuickBooks 103

Company Snapshot 118

Budgeting and Forecasting 121
Steps to Create Budget in QuickBooks 122
Steps to Create Forecasts in QuickBooks 123

PART THREE

Learning Objectives (Quickbooks Case Study) 125

PART FOUR

Appendix A: List Of A Standard Chart Of Accounts 184

Appendix A: List ofa Standard Chart of Accounts 184

The 20 Key QuickBooks Keyboard Shortcuts 197

From the Author 198

Useful Sources 199

Introduction

Over the years, more and more people have turned to QuickBooks for business and financial purposes. Intuit QuickBooks launched its first version in 1992 for both the IBM PC on Microsoft DOS and Apple's Macintosh systems.

Now, there are more than 4 million global QuickBooks users throughout many versions. This is the most of any accounting-based business software vendor in history. Due to its ease and simple user interface, QuickBooks is extremely cost-effective for all types of businesses.

This book will teach you the fundamental accounting principles and how to apply them confidently in real life situations; basic logistics of personal and business day-to-day bookkeeping; how to master the full accounting cycle by solving real-world projects and cases; how to master the basics of QuickBooks (from simple editing to making reports); and how to familiarize yourself with shortcuts, everyday business forms, and templates that are directly generated from QuickBooks Accounting Software.

If you'd like to learn or improve your financial and accounting skills (whether you're a business student, business owner, financial analyst, or just a financial enthusiast), this book is right for you. This book teaches you how to use QuickBooks, explains accounting concepts, and demonstrates each section with applicable real-world situations.

About the author

Fraidun Besharat is an MBA degree holder from the Cumberland University in Tennessee, U.S. and has not only collaboratively published several other books but has also held various positions as a business financial analyst and accountant. With his expertise, Besharat has helped over 150 small and medium-sized enterprises (SMEs) on their accounting and financial system, bookkeeping policy and producer, business planning, as well as contributed to the growth of various industries both at the domestic and international levels. Additionally, he has also worked as a lecturer at universities and coached others on matters e-commerce.

Significant things covered in this book

This is a complete, comprehensive, step-by-step guide on how to use QuickBooks as an accountant or business manager, business owner, or for personal means. This book is precise and completely practical-oriented.

There are many real-world examples in this book, which is why it is unique. These scenarios make it easier to implement what you have learned and will teach you how to tackle any situation that may arise when using QuickBooks. This book will also serve as a reference if you come across such real-world situations later in your career.

This book is divided into four parts:

- **Part one:** Fundamental accounting and bookkeeping
- **Part two:** Overview and deep understanding of QuickBooks 2020
- **Part three:** Solving and applying real-world case in QuickBooks
- **Part four:** Appendixes, forms and templates

This book covers all areas of QuickBooks usage and more, including:

- Fundamental accounting principles and how to apply them
- Confidently handling both personal and business day-to-day

bookkeeping.
- Completing the full accounting cycle by solving real-world project cases.
- Getting started with QuickBooks homepage, file, edit, view, list, company, customers, vendors, employees, banking, and reports.
- Completing the full accounting cycle in QuickBooks by applying real-world project cases.
- Familiarizing with various shortcuts, everyday business forms, and templates directly generated from QuickBooks Accounting Software.

The number one problem in today's generation and economy is the lack of financial literacy.

Alan Greenspan

PART (I)

Fundamental Accounting

The Bookkeeping and Double Entry

Accounting

Bookkeeping

Accrual vs. Cash Basis of Accounting

The Accounts

The Accounting Equation

Debit and Credit

Some Everyday Use of Debit and Credit

Journal Entries

T-Accounts

Adjusting Entry

General Ledger

Summary of The Accounting Cycle

Petty Cash

Bank Reconciliation

Financial Statements

Recording Transactions in Balance Sheet

Accounts Receivable and Payable

Preparing Income Statement

Depreciation

Preparing Cash Flow Statement

Relation of Depreciation and Financial Statements

Depreciation Methods

Real-World Example to Complete Accounting Cycle

Bookkeeping and Double Ent

Learning Objectives (Fundamental Accounting)

The Bookkeeping and Double Entry

■ Defining accounting

Accounting is simply identifying, measuring, classifying, verifying, summarizing, recording, and interpreting financial information to help management make better business and financial decisions. Since the purpose of accounting is to record, summarize, and provide financial business data to different users of such data, it is necessary to have some means to achieve that goal. One of these means is called the account.

■ Defining Bookkeeping

Bookkeeping includes the regular reporting of financial transactions and the preservation of the organization's accurate and up-to-date financial records. With proper bookkeeping, companies can track all business information in the company's books. This helps the company make significant decisions, including operating, investing, and financing related matters. Bookkeepers are individuals that manage and maintain all the financial data for companies. Therefore, without bookkeepers, companies would have no clue about their current financial position and any transactions that occur within the company.

Fundamental Accounting
Bookkeeping and double entry

Accrual vs. Cash Basis of Accounting

This can be defined as the Cash Basis of Accounting. This type of accounting is only done when there is a transaction that involves cash payment or expenditure. As a result, there is no existence of accounts receivable and accounts payable. However, in the Accrual Basis of Accounting, transactions are recorded even if the Cash is not received or paid and vice versa. There would be accounts receivable and accounts payable.

Before implementing any financial system, the companies need to choose the accounting method that will be applied. Companies can choose between two basic accounting methods: cash basis of accounting or accrual basis of accounting. As stated above, the only thing that differentiates these two accounting methods is based on when the company records the sales (money inflow) and purchases or expenses (money outflow) in the journal book.

The Accounts

Five main accounts are used to keep track of financial transactions. However, the type of accounts is not limited to these as there are hundreds of other sub-accounts to these main account types. This is also called a standard chart of accounts in companies.

- Asset
- Liability
- Capital or Shareholder's Equity
- Revenue
- Expense

From the accounts stated above, asset, liability, and capital or shareholder's equity are the balance sheet components. However, revenue and expense are the components of the income statement or statement of profit and loss.

The Accounting Equation

The accounting equation follows the basic principle of accounting and fundamental elements of the balance sheet. So, the equation is as

Fundamental Accounting

Bookkeeping and double entry

follows:

$$\text{Assets} = \text{Liabilities} + \text{Shareholder's Equity}$$

Example of each part of the equation or balance sheet:

Assets: Cash and Bank, Accounts Receivable, Inventory, Equipment

Liabilities: Accounts Payable, Short-term Borrowings, Long-term Debt

Shareholder's Equity: Share Capital, Retained Earnings

This equation is the foundation of double-entry accounting and highlights the structure of the balance sheet.

However, if the Shareholder's Equity is unclear in the company, we can find it through rearranging into the following form to get the capital.

$$\text{Capital or Shareholder's Equity} = \text{Assets} - \text{Liabilities}$$

So, regardless of how the accounting equation is represented, it is essential to remember that the equation must always be a balance.

For every transaction, both sides of this equation must have an equal net effect. Below are some examples of transactions and how they affect the accounting equation. Also, this is known as the balance of scale.

Example (1) Cash

Company XYZ wishes to purchase a $350 Lab machine using only Cash. This transaction would result in a Debit to Equipment (+$350) and a Credit to Cash (-$350). The net effect on the accounting equation would be as follows:

Assets	=	Liabilities	+	Shareholder's Equity
+350				
-350	=	0	+	0

This transaction affects the assets sides only on the equation; therefore, there is no similar effect in liabilities or capital equity on the right side of the equation.

Example (2) Credit

Company XYZ wishes to purchase a $400 machine, but it only has $200 of

Fundamental Accounting

Bookkeeping and double entry

Cash in its holdings. The company can purchase this machine with an initial payment of $200, but it owes the manufacturer the remaining amount. This would result in a Debit to Equipment (+4500), a credit to Accounts Payable (+$200), and a Debit to Cash (-$200). The net effect on the accounting equation would be as follows:

Asset	=	Liabilities	+	Capital
+400	=	+200		
-200				
+200	=	+200	+	0

Defining Debit and Credit

Assets: Debit increase and Credit decrease

Liabilities: Credit increase and Debit decrease

Capital: Credit increase and Debit decrease

Revenue: Credit increase and Debit decrease

Expense: Debit increase and Credit decrease

Some Everyday Use Of Debit And Credit:

- If you start investing in the company in Cash: Cash or bank is on the Debit (Dr) side, and investment account or equity is on the Credit (Cr) side.
- If you are the owner and want to withdraw money from the company for personal uses: Investment withdrawal is recorded on the Debit (Dr), and Cash is recorded on the Credit (Cr).
- If sales occur in Cash, a Bank or cash account is recorded on the Debit side, and Sales or revenue will be Credit.
- If sales occur on Credit, the accounts receivable will be Debit (Dr), and the revenue account will be Credit (Cr).

Fundamental Accounting
Bookkeeping and double entry

- If Customer paid as account receivable: Cash or bank will be Debit (Dr), and account receivable will be Credit (Cr).
- If Office supplies purchased in Cash: Office supplies will be Debit (Dr), and Cash or Bank will be Credit (Cr).
- If Office supplies purchased on Credit: Office supplies expense will be Debit (Dr) and account payable to that supplier will be Credit (Cr).
- If the item purchased for inventory purpose is in Cash: Inventory will be Debit (Dr), and Cash or bank will be Credit (Cr).
- If the item for inventory purpose is purchased on Credit: Inventory will be Debit (Dr) and account payable will be Credit (Cr).
- If the company pays salary/wages to employees: Salary or wages expense will be Debit (Dr), and Cash or bank will be Credit (Cr).
- If you take a loan from a lender or bank: Cash or bank will be Debit, and loan payable (short/long term) will be Credit (Cr).
- If you decide to pay back the loan: Loan payable will be Debit (Dr), and Cash or bank will be Credit (Cr).

From the statements above, we understand a Debit (Dr) is an accounting entry that either increases an asset or expense on the left side of an account or decreases a liability or equity account. A Credit (Cr) is an accounting entry that either increases a liability or equity account or decreases an asset or expense positioning on the right side of an account.

It would be better not to forget that Debit and Credit are not associated with plus or minus but, the reality is that Debit simply means left and Credit means right. In some cases, you've probably seen that "Debit" is abbreviated as "Dr." and "credit," "Cr." in the T-accounts.

Journal Entries

A journal is the company's official financial book in which all transactions are recorded in chronological order. Nowadays, most companies use accounting software such as QB to book journal entries. In every journal entry that is recorded, the Debit and Credit must be equal to ensure that the accounting equation remains balanced "Assets = Liabilities + Owner's Equity."

In order to do proper GJE, the following factors should be under consideration:

- When accounts are affected by the transaction.
- For each account, determine if it is increased or decreased.
- For each account, determined by how much it changed.
- Ensure that the accounting equation stays in balance.

T-Accounts

From the accounting perspective, *T-account* is another form of the ledger that represents all account as an individual. Therefore, it is called T-account because it looks like the English letter (T) where the left side represents Debit and the right side, Credit. For various accounts, debits and credits can mean either an increase or a decrease, but in a T-Account, the Debit is always on the left side, and Credit is always on the right side by convention.

Adjusting Entry

This type of entries is required at the end of each fiscal period to align the revenues and expenses to the right period due to the matching principle in accounting. There are two types of adjusting entry: *accruals* and *deferrals*. Adjusting entry, generally, occurs before the financial Statement is released.

- Accruals, revenues earned, or expenses incurred that have not been previously recorded.
- Deferrals, receipts of assets, or payments of Cash in advance of revenue or expense recognition.

Deferred revenue: When Cash is received prior to earning revenue by delivering goods/services, the company records a journal entry to recognize unearned revenue.

Deferred revenue is the portion of a company's revenue that has not been earned, but Cash has been collected from customers in the form of prepayment.

Accrued revenue: When revenue is earned but not recorded at the end of the accounting period because cash changes hands after the service are performed, or goods are delivered.

Fundamental Accounting
Bookkeeping and double entry

Accrued revenue is revenue that has been earned by providing a good or service to customers, but for which no cash has been received.

Deferred expense: Amount paid in advance for using assets that benefit more than one period.

Accrued expense: The process of recognizing expenses before the Cash is paid.

An accrued expense is a liability that represents an expense that has been recognized but not yet paid. A deferred expense is an asset that represents a prepayment of future expenses that have not yet been incurred.

General Ledger

General Ledger is a complete record of all financial transactions that occur in the company through its lifetime. The General Ledger is a supporter to prepare trial balance easily. If you want to see how the cash flow of a company has changed over time and all its relevant transactions, you will look at the general ledger, which shows all the debit and credit transactions.

This was done on paperback then, but, fortunately, new technologies such as QuickBooks, Sage, etc. made accounting easier.

Summary of the Accounting Cycle

- *Transaction:* Include a debt payoff, purchases, depreciation, sales, expenses, or a new investment, etc.
- *Journal Entry:* Double-entry or Debiting one or more accounts and Crediting one or more accounts, and this rule must always be aligned.
- *Posting to GL:* This process is where a summary of various accounts split into individual related accounts. For instance, all accounts payable should be summarized under one main account.
- *Trial Balance:* All the total balance of general ledger accounts was calculated either with Debit or Credit.
- *Worksheet:* If Dr or Cr on the trial balance does not match, the accountant must look for an error in the worksheet and track any
- *Adjusting Entries:* At the end of every accounting period, for instance, monthly closing, the adjusting entry on accounts accruals

and deferrals should be posted.

- *Financial Statement:* After adjustments are made and balances are corrected, the income statement and balance can be prepared.
- *Closing:* The revenue and expense accounts are zeroed and closed out for the next accounting cycle. Revenue and expense accounts are components of an income statement account, which tells the operational performance of an entity in a specific period. Since the balance sheet tells the company's financial position at a certain point in time, this is a closed instead of carried balance to the next period. The accounting closing process (also called "closing the books") is the start of the next accounting period.

Petty Cash

Petty Cash is a small amount of Cash that is kept on the company premises to pay for minor cash needs. It depends on the size of the company, but usually the Cash between $50-$1500 can be adjustable. This is also used to reimburse employees for small expenses. Of course, petty Cash is under the current asset category.

Bank Reconciliation

Bank reconciliation is the process of creating reports used to check and explain the differences or variances between the cash balance in the company's ledger account and bank balance shown in the bank statement. The process includes the following:

- Begin with the bank's ending cash balance.
- Add any deposits in transit.
- Deduct any cheques that have not been cleared yet, such as pending cheques.
- The company's ending cash balance with deductions for any bank charges fee or penalties and additions for any interest gained.
- The adjusted bank balance should be equal to the company's ending adjusted cash balance.

Financial Statements

Financial statements are records of the financial activities of a business.

There are three key financial statements:

Balance sheet: Also known as Statement of financial position. In short, the balance sheet shows what the company owns, what it owes, and what it's worth. The main components of the balance sheet are as follows:

a) **Assets**
- Current assets (Cash, inventory, account receivable, prepaid…etc.)
- Non-current assets (PPE or property, plant, and equipment, brand name, software)

b) **Liabilities (what the company owes)**
- Current liabilities (due within a year such as any short-term payables)
- Non-current liabilities (due more than a year such as long-term debt or payable)

c.) Equity (what the business is worth with debt & liabilities, or losses deducted such as commons shares and retained earnings)

The concept on the above is that this equation should be in balance *(Assets= Liabilities + Equity)* and in order to find the owners net worth, *Equality =Assets – Liabilities)*

Income statement: Shows what a company has earned, what it has paid, and the resulting profit or losses over a specific period. The main components of the income statement are as follows:
- Revenue
- Expenses
- Profit and Loss

Statement of cash flows: Show cash movement of business like how much Cash the company has brought in, and how much it has paid out. The main components of the cash flow statement are as follows:

Fundamental Accounting

Bookkeeping and double entry

- Cash flow from operating activities
- Cash flow from investing activities
- Cash flow from financing activities

Recording Transactions in Balance Sheet

In order to record in the balance sheet, the principle here is that the balance sheet should always be in balance and apply for a double-entry - bookkeeping accounting system (Debit and Credit):

a) Recording transactions on both sides of the balance sheet. For instance: Pay off your debt in Cash by $200. This is how it is recorded in the balance sheet:

- *Current asset* (Cash by $200 decreased in balance sheet left side)
- *Liabilities* (Short-term Loan by $200 also decreased in balance sheet right side)

b) Recording transactions on the same side of the balance sheet both (+/-) number. For instance: If you make an asset purchase like a computer laptop for $500 and pay in Cash. The fixed asset will be increased by $500 on the left side of the balance sheet, and the current asset (Cash) will be decreased by $500.

Note: If you construct a balance sheet with the above transaction, you will find that all are balanced on both sides.

Example:

Zoivu Co. is a small business firm that has done some financial activities, as stated below. As the accountant, record the following items in order to build the balance sheet:

- The company issued out $500 shares in Cash.
- Took out an eight-year loan of $300 from a financial firm.
- Purchased PP&E for $200.
- Purchased item for inventory at $250.
- The company sold the entire inventory items for $300 in Cash and 50% on credit.
- The bi-weekly employee salaries have been directly deposited for $400.
- The interest charged on the financial loan paid for $50.

Fundamental Accounting

Bookkeeping and double entry

ASSETS		LIABILITIES	
Current assets		**Current liabilities**	
Cash (500+300-200-250+150-400-50	$50	Loans payable and long-term debt	$
Short-term investments		Accounts payable and accrued exp	$
Accounts receivable	$150		
Inventories (250-250)	$-	Total current liabilities	$ -
Prepaid expenses and other exp	$-	**Non-current liabilities**	
Total current assets	$200	Long-term debt (8 years bank loan)	$300
Fixed assets		Deferred income taxes	$
Property, plant, and equipment at cost	$200	Deferred credits and other liabilities	$
Less accumulated depreciation			
Total fixed assets	$200		
Other assets			
Long-term cash investments	$		
Equity investments	$		
Deferred income taxes	$	Total other liabilities	$300
Other assets	$	Total liabilities	$300
Total other assets	$ -	Total owners' equity	$100
Total assets	$400	Total liabilities + owners' equity	$400

Fundamental Accounting
Bookkeeping and double entry

Accounts Receivable and Payable

Accounts receivable is the amount owed by the customer to the company. In contrast, the accounts payable is the amount owed by the company to suppliers. Hence, if the purchases and sales are both made on credit, the accrual basis of accounting system applies.

Preparing an Income Statement

The income statement is also known as the statement of operations and statement of Profit and loss (P&L) that shows the company's financial result from the operational perspective.

A. The income statement format:

- **Revenue:** The income statement starts with the **Revenue**, sales, or turnover.
- **Direct Operating Cost:** Such as Cost of goods sold (COGS).
- **Gross Profit:** The third after deducting Cost of selling the (Revenue – COGS) the result would be as **Gross Profit** or at some point, also called Margin. In Margin, the (selling price – minus landed Cost of the product).
- **Indirect Operating Cost:** Such as R&D, general administration expense, selling, and Distribution Cost.
- **Operating Income (EBIT):** Fifth would be listed in the income statement as **the operating income**
- **is common (EBIT)**, which stands for Earnings
- Before Interest and Taxes.
- **Cost of Debt Financing:** The sixth item list in the income statement includes interest charges, bank charges, or late fees.
- **Tax:** Deduct the tax from the Profit or sales depending on the state law or country income tax law such as 2% or 20%.
- **Net Income Before Tax:** The format of income statement is flexible, but according to GAAP, this stands for General Accounting Accepted Principle.
- **Net Income After Tax:** Final net Profit or losses after all expenses, costs, and taxes are deducted. It is very important to remember that the retained earnings always move to the

Fundamental Accounting

Bookkeeping and double entry

balance sheet to either increase or decrease the owner's equity, depending on the nature of negative or positive.

B. Record Transactions

- Zoiv Co. has done some activities and asks you to record the items to prepare an income statement. All the items that we are going to track on the income statement will ultimately be combined to create the accounts that flow into retained earnings, which would be Net Income.

- Purchased an item for inventory $250

- The company has sold the entire inventory items for $300 in cash and 50% on credit

- The bi-weekly employee salary has been directly deposited for $400

- The interest charged on the financial loan paid for $50

Income Statement

Revenue	$300
COGS	($250)
Gross Profit	$50
Selling &Admin. Expenses	($400)
Operating Profit	($50)
Interest and Tax Expenses	$0
Net Profit	**($400)**

Recording income statements should only be included in the revenues and expenses related to the accounting fiscal year.

Example (1):

Last month, the company decided to purchase 12 months of insurance for the entire year at the Cost of $600. How much insurance would be included in the P&L?

Because the insurance covers the entire year, only one of the 12 months ($50) should be recorded in the income statement. What will happen for the remaining 11 months? The answer for the rest is $550, but it should be recorded in the balance sheet as a prepaid expense under the current asset.

Fundamental Accounting

Bookkeeping and double entry

The recording should look like this:

No	Transaction Details	Accounts	Debit	Credit
1	Prepaid insurance for 11 months Cash	Balance Sheet Bank/Cash	$550	$550
2	Insurance Expense Cash	Expense Bank/Cash	$50	$50
			$600	$600

Some office supplies were used in the current fiscal year, but not paid for until the year after. The supplies were worth $1000. Now, how much of this expense should be included in the income statement for this year? The answer: All that $1000 expense should be included in the income statement, as this is the value of the office suppliers used in the current fiscal year.

This is an accrued expense to be recorded in the balance sheet due to the payment not having been made yet. An accrued expense has been reflected as an expense in the income statement that hasn't been paid yet.

Accrued expense should be recorded under current liabilities in the balance sheet for $1000 as the following double entry:

No	Transaction Details	Accounts	Debit	Credit
1	Office Supplies Expense Accrued Expense	Expense Current Liabilities/Balance Sheet	$1000	$1000

Depreciation

The Zoivu Co. has purchased a PP&E for the value of $200, and we now assume that the useful life of this equipment estimates up to five years. We could allocate usefulness evenly over the years of use, which is five years. The equipment has a **scrap value** (also called the **residual value**) of $20.

- The reduction of PP&E value over the course of five years will be

Fundamental Accounting

Bookkeeping and double entry

recorded as a depreciation expense.

- ➤ We use a simple formula to calculate:
- ➤ **Depreciation cost = purchase price − scrap value/useful life.**
- ➤ Apply the above equipment into the formula:
- ➤ **Depreciation = $200-$20/5 = $36 per year (for five years)**
- ➤ The result ($36) will be recorded in the income statement under depreciation expense for the next five years.

- The following should be recorded in the **balance sheet**:
    - ➤ The PPE&E should be recorded in the balance sheet as a balance:
    - ➤ PP&E = Purchase price − depreciation expense = Closing balance.
    - ➤ The PP&E closing balance = $200 − 36 = $164 (this is the value of PP&E at the end of first year in the balance sheet after deducting depreciation expense) $164 is the beginning balance for the next year:
        - $200- $36 = $164
        - $164 -36 = $128
        - $128- 36 = $92
        - $92 - $36 = $56
        - $56 -$36 = $20 (estimated scrap value or residual value at fifth year)
        - What will happen to the **scrap value** or **salvage value** of $20?
        - If the company decides to sell that PP&E at the fifth-year end at the price point of $20, then that value should be recorded in the income statement as a sales/income and removed from the balance sheet.

However, if the asset is not sold and remains in the balance sheet, then the value should remain the same as $20.

Preparing Cash Flow Statement

In this section, we will learn how the cash flow statement format looks, the difference between cash flow and income statement, and how to construct a cash flow statement by utilizing income statements and balance sheets.

All cash items could be recorded in the balance sheet as a "closing cash balance." However, all the other cash details are shown in cash flow statements, as mentioned earlier. The cash flow organizes the cash inflow and cash outflow in three main categories:

1. Details for cash flow from operating activities
    - Revenues, operating expenses: It only includes the Revenue that the company has incurred or received the cash for and consists of the expenses which the company paid the cash out.
2. Details for cash flow from **investment activities**
    - **Sales/purchases of assets**: Includes selling of property plant and equipment or purchasing of PP&E, investing, or acquiring other businesses.
3. Details for cash flow from **financing activities**
    - **Issuing shares, raising debt**: Repurchasing or repaying debt or paying dividends.

Understanding where cash comes from and where it is used are both very significant processes to business managers, financial analysts, owners, and other users of the financial statement.

Relation of Depreciation and Financial Statements

Zoivu Co. purchases a vehicle for $20,000 and will use it in the business for five years. In another five years, they anticipate reselling it for $5000 as residual/scrap value.

What should the company show in the cash flow statement, income

Fundamental Accounting

Bookkeeping and double entry

statement, and balance sheet?

There are two possibilities to think about:

1. The company uses the straight-line method of Depreciation.
2. The company books a full year of Depreciation expense in the year it makes the purchase.

Solution: Remember the accounting principle of recognizing, classifying, and recording. The following accounts will be reflected as a result of this Depreciation transaction:

a. **Balance sheet**

- Assets: Since PP&E is an asset category, the total of $20,000 will be recorded in the balance sheet, and the Depreciation keeps deducting the value every year to reach $5000 salvage value.
- Liabilities
- Equity

b. **Income Statement**

- Revenues
- Expenses: Total $20,000 "purchase cost fraction" − $5000 (salvage value)/5years (useful life) = $3,000
- (will be booked as a Depreciation expense for each year until reaching crap value at fifth year)
- Profit and Loss

c. **Cash Flow Statement**

- Operating Activities
- Investing Activities: The total value of PP&E $20,000 will be recorded in cash outflow from investing activities as capital expenditure.
- Financing Activities

Depreciation Methods

There are several depreciation methods that you can apply while calculating Depreciation on your company's or personal fixed assets (except for the land and intangible assets).

These are listed beginning with the most common and simple method as the following:

- **Straight-line method:** An equal amount of Depreciation is applied every year to the asset's useful life.
- **Double declining balance method:** It's a form of accelerated Depreciation where the depreciation expense is excellent in the first several years and smaller in the later years. This method can be used for a company that wants to lower its tax bill in the early years by having a bigger depreciation expense that lowers the tax bill.
- **Units of production method**: The depreciation expense varies each year and is based on the output produced by the asset. This method of Depreciation is useful to the company that wants to match the actual production of the business to the Depreciation expense that incurs.

The following is how the formulas for each of these methods should be presented:

- *Straight-line Depreciation*= Cost or initial purchase – salvage value/useful life of asset X
- *Double declining balance*= 100%/useful life of asset X beginning period of book value
- *Unit of production depreciation* = Number of produced/lifetime number of unit X(cost-salvage value).

Bookkeeping

The purpose of proper business or personal bookkeeping is to create a record of financial transactions that are organized in such a way that allows business owners and accounting professionals to analyze the business financial data and prepare financial reports for better decision making and taxes. However, these transactions are managed in the chart of accounts, known as the backbone of accounting system.

Fundamental Accounting
Bookkeeping and double entry

Some Posting and Non-posting Transactions

1. Expense (Posting)
2. This is the transaction form to pay suppliers or vendors who provide goods and services using cash, check, or credit card at the time of making purchases.
3. Check (Posting)
4. This is the transaction form to pay vendors using check only at the time of purchase.
5. Bill (Non-Posting)
6. This is common in an accrual basis of accounting transaction forms to record expense on payment for those services or goods provided from a supplier to companies on credit.
7. Pay Bills (Posting)
8. This is a payment transaction to record payment of previous bills entered in the system or in other ways that the purchase was made on credit.
9. Purchase Order (Non-Posting)
10. This is an accounting transaction form that is used to request and track supplier purchases and goods or services history.
11. Vendor credit (Posting)
12. This is an accounting transaction form used to record returns to suppliers and vendors or obtains refunds from them.
13. Credit card credit (Posting)
14. This is an accounting transaction form to record the return of expense processed through a credit card account.
15. Sales receipt (Posting)
16. This is an accounting transaction form used for payment at the time of making sales.
17. An Invoice Vs. Bill (Posting)
18. This is a sales form that allows your clients who haven't met a sales deadline to agree on later terms. Always remember this basic rule when creating invoices that you earn the income, but no cash has been received yet. Moreover, creating an invoice increases the

Fundamental Accounting
Bookkeeping and double entry

accounts receivable. However, this is opposite for Bills.

Some Key Bookkeeping Checklist

These checklists help you navigate through every step of accounting process in different time period in order to have a proper bookkeeping and accounting record:

Daily Checklist

- The daily task is to make sure you have enough funds on your account, as this is a critical part of business in order to be able to operate your daily business and know that you're not running out of cash.

Weekly Checklist

- **Recording transactions**: These transactions can be anything in order to have a better picture on your money in and out of the business, such as customer invoice and payment, vendor billing, and payments.
- **Documenting and Filing**: These help you keep the confidential supporting document of the transaction that you made (contracts, invoice, bills, etc.)
- **Review Unpaid Bills**: You can do this by making a list of all unpaid bills to your vendor, including the payment amount and due date.
- **Preparing and Sending Invoices**: If you want to have always a positive cash flow, you need to keep up with your customer for receiving payments on time.
- **Projected Flow of Cash**: Develop a spreadsheet to understand how much cash is coming and going weekly from different sources.

Monthly Checklist

- **Balancing Checkbook**: Assure cash transaction entries are accurate and have an accurate cash position.
- **Review and Follow Past Aging**: Keep track of your expecting receivables from your customer by sending a reminder to collect money.
- **Checking and updating inventory**: Make sure you have enough items in stock to fulfill your purchase order.
- **Paying Salaries/Payroll**: Make sure your employees are getting paid and taxes are withheld and paid to appropriate tax collection.

Fundamental Accounting

Bookkeeping and double entry

- **Understanding your P&L and Balance Sheet vs. Budget:** You can create and develop your budget monthly, quarterly, half year, and annual budget and compare them with the actual profit and loss in the company to understand where you stand.

Quarterly Checklist:

- **File Estimated Taxes**: In order to prevent any fines and penalties, proactively pay the estimated quarterly taxes. This also helps lower your year-end tax.

- **Review and Sales Tax Payment**: Depending on the state you are operating in; you need to comply with rules and regulations if they require sales tax.

- **Review Payroll Reports**: Regarding taxes, you deal with IRS and state rules and regulations and check with your local tax agency to making sure that taxes are logged on payroll reports and payment properly.

- **Prepare Annual P&L Estimate**: Once you start a business operating by making sales and occurring expenses, then you can evaluate several months to estimate an annual P&L accordingly by deducting revenue from the cost and expenses.

Annual Checklist:

- **Review Overdue Receivable (Aging):** See all "pending payment invoices list" and determine whether you need to send customers a follow-up reminder or refer to a collection agency. If this is outdated, offset for the tax purpose.

- **W-2 and 1099 MISC**: Every first day of the second month of the year is the deadline for the report annual earnings of both W-2 and contractor employees.

- **Inventory review**: Inventory is a current asset and you need to do valuation of your inventory that hasn't been sold yet and use unsellable inventory as a deduction for yearend tax purposes.

- **Prepare and review both financial reports and tax returns**: This checklist helps you act proactively and be ahead of the game in terms of your tax preparation and documentation reporting to internal revenue services.

Real-World Example To Complete Accounting Cycle

Bookkeeping and Double Entry

The following consists of 24 real-world examples to complete the accounting cycle. As you learned from the beginning, the accounting cycle consists of several steps to have accurate and appropriate records. They are the following:

- Occurring financial transactions
- Making journal entries in the book
- Posting entries from journal to general ledger
- Preparing and building a trial balance called "Un-adjusted, Adjusting, Adjusted TBs"
- Preparing and organizing the financial statements, "P&L, Balance Sheet, Cash flow, Equity"
- Closing the account.

Fundamental Accounting

Real-world Example to complete accounting cycle

Below is an accounting cycle process:

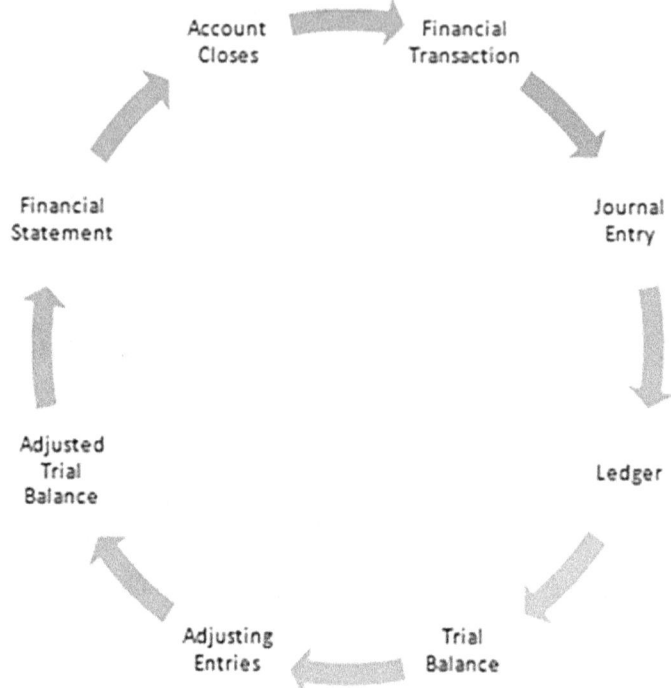

Example of Real-world Case with Solutions

Zoivu Co., a business firm, had some financial transactions in February 2020 recorded with the consideration of all accounting principles, rules, and regulations:

Suppose Zoivu Co. started a business operation at the beginning of March 2020 and the following financial transaction occurred in the company:

1. Mar. 1, 2020: The company starts with an initial investment of $300,000 cash deposited in a Bank of America checking account and a building for the value of $2,000,000 in the business. The owner's name is Frank.

2. Mar. 2, 2020: The company decides to purchase $5,000 worth of computer and equipment online from Amazon and payment is entirely processed through the checking account.

3. Mar. 3, 2020: Furniture and fixture for office use purchased on

Fundamental Accounting
Real-world Example to complete accounting cycle

credit at $3,000 for a 15-day payment plan from Home Depot.

4. Mar. 5, 2020: Nissan car purchased for daily office operation that cost $35,000, 50% of which is paid in cash and the remaining due over the next 12 months in credit.

5. Mar. 6, 2020: Insurance expense ($1,000 from checking account) paid to GEICO until Mar. 6, 2021.

6. Mar. 7, 2020: Sales made to Sky company for providing logistic services and earned $32,000. Deposited into checking account.

7. Mar. 7, 2020: Frank (owner of the company) decides to create a new cash account "Petty Cash" to reimburse and process daily operational costs and transfers $50,000 cash from checking account.

8. Mar. 10, 2020: Frank withdraws $500 from Petty Cash for his personal expense.

9. Mar. 12, 2020: The new car is filled at the gas station and is paid via cash ($50).

10. Mar. 15, 2020: Sales made on credit for the services amounts for $10,000 to Company ABC, who agrees to pay in the next 10 days.

11. Mar. 20, 2020: The new car is sent to the mechanic for a checkup. Cost: $200 in cash

12. Mar. 25, 2020: Internet bill arrives for the month of March. Cost: $150, paid via checking account.

13. Mar. 30, 2020: ABC pays the collectible invoice for $10,000 and deposits it into the checking account.

14. Mar. 31, 2020: The company receives a bill for bank charges of $50 from Bank of America, which is paid through the checking account.

15. Mar. 31, 2020: Depreciation expense booked in the company for all depreciable fixed assets.

Note: Complete accounting cycle and prepare financial statements at the end of the period (Month).

Fundamental Accounting

Real-world Example to complete accounting cycle

1. Entry in General Journal

Zoivu Logistic Co
General Journal
Mar 31, 2020

Date	Amount	Ref	Debit	Credit
2020 Mar 1	Bank Building Frank Capital *Initial Investment from Frank*		$300,000 $2,000,000	$2,300,000
Mar 2	Computer Bank *Purchased computer and equipment*		$5,000	$5,000
Mar 3	Furniture & Fixture Accounts Payable *Purchased fixed assets on credit for 15 days terms from Home Depot*		$3,000	$3,000
Mar 5	Vehicle Cash Accounts Payable *Purchased vehicle in cash and credit for the next 12 months*		$35,000	$17,500 $17,500
Mar 6	Insurance prepaid expense Bank *Purchased insurance and paid for the next one year*		$1,000	$1,000
Mar 7	Bank Service Sales *Sales made in cash to Sky company*		$32,000	$32,000
Mar 7	Petty Cash Bank *Fund transfer made from Bank account to Petty cash*		$50,000	$50,000
Mar 10	Frank Withdrawal Petty Cash *Owner withdrawal for personal expense*		$500	$500
Mar 12	Gas expense Petty Cash *Gas expense for new car*		$50	$50
Mar 12	Account Receivable Service Sales *Sales made on credit to ABC company within 10 days payment terms*		$10,000	$10,000
Mar 20	Repair and Maintenance Petty Cash *New car tested technically to run well*		$200	$200

Fundamental Accounting

Real-world Example to complete accounting cycle

Mar 25	Internet expense Bank *Utility bill for internet paid*		$100	$100
Mar 30	Bank Account Receivable *AR collected from ABC company and deposited in Bank*		$10,000	$10,000
Mar 31	Bank Charges Expense Bank *Bank maintenance fee for the monthly statement BOA*		$50	$50
Mar 31	Depreciation Expense Accumulated Depreciation *Depreciation on fixed assets*		$600	$600
Mar 31	Salary Expense Bank *Staff Salary for the month*		$4,500	$4,500

2. Posting in Ledger (T-Accounts):

Bank	
$ 300,000	$ 5,000
$ 32,000	$ 1,000
$ 10,000	$ 50,000
	$ 100
	$ 50
	$ 4,500
$ 281,350.00	

Cash	
$ 50,000	$ 17,500
	$ 500
	$ 50
	$ 200
$ 31,750.00	

Accumulated Depreciation	
$ -	$ 600
	$ 600.00

Service sales	
-	$ 32,000
	$ 42,000.00

Fundamental Accounting

Real-world Example to complete accounting cycle

Continue Posting in Ledger

Frank Capital	
$ -	$ 2,300,000
	$ 2,300,000.00

Accounts Payable	
$ -	$ 17,500
	$ 3,000
	$ 20,500.00

Withdrawal	
$ 500	$ -
$ 500.00	

Building	
$ 2,000,000	$ -
$ 2,000,000.00	

Accounts Receivable	
$ 10,000	$ 10,000
-$ -	

Computer Equipment	
$ 5,000.00	$ -
$ 5,000.00	

Vehicle	
$ 35,000.00	$ -
$ 35,000.00	

Prepaid Expense	
$ 1,000	$ -
$ 1,000.00	

Insurance Expense	
$ 83	$ -
$ 83.33	

Fundamental Accounting

Real-world Example to complete accounting cycle

Continue Posting in Ledger

Depreciation Expense	
$ 600	$ -
$ 600.00	

Furniture & Fixture	
$ 3,000	$ -
$ 3,000	

Gas Expense	
$ 50	$ -
	$
$ 50.00	

Repair Expense	
$ 200	$ -
	$
$ 200.00	

Internet Expense	
$ 100	$ -
	$
$ 200.00	

Bank Charges Expense	
$ 50	$ -
	$
$ 50.00	

Salary Expense	
$ 4,500	$ -
	$
$ 4,500.00	

3. Preparing Trial Balance, Adjusting Entry, Adjusted Trail Balance (USD)

- Un-adjusted trial balance
- Adjusting entries
- Adjusted trial balance

Fundamental Accounting

Real-world Example to complete accounting cycle

Zoivu Logistic Co.
Trial Balances, Adjusting, and Adjusted Trial Balance
Mar. 31, 2020

Account	Trial Balance		Adjusting Entries		Adjusted Trial Balance	
	Debit	Credit	Debit	Credit	Debit	Credit
Services Sales		42,000			-	42,000
Depreciation Expense	600	-			600	-
Gas Expense	50				50	-
Insurance Expense			83		83	-
Repair & Maintenance	200				200	-
Internet Charges	100				100	-
Bank Charges	50				50	-
Salary Expense	4500					
Prepaid Expense	1000			83	917	83
Frank Investment		2,300,000			-	2,300,000
Frank Withdrawal	500				500	-
Ac Frank Withdrawal		20,500			-	20,500
Accumulated Depreciation		600			-	600
Bank	281,350				285,850	-
Cash	31,750				31,750	-
Accounts Receivable	-					-
Building	2,000,000				2,000,000	-
Furniture and Fixture	3,000				3,000	-
Computer & Equipment	5,000				5,000	-
Vehicle	35,000				35,000	-
Total Debit & Credit 2,363,183 (USD)	2,363,100	2,363,100	83	83	2,363,183	2,363,183

Fundamental Accounting

Real-world Example to complete accounting cycle

In order to prove that our accounting and financial transactions recorded appropriately in trial balance, you can see that both sides of total debit and credit equally balanced at $2,363,183.

4. Preparing Income Statement (P&L)

Zoivu Logistic Co. Profit and Loss (P&L) 31-Mar-20	
Revenue from services	42,000
Other sales	-
Discount	-
Total Net Revenue	**42,000**
Cost of Goods Sold	-
Gross Profit	**42,000**
Expenses	
Depreciation & Amortization	600
Insurance	83
Maintenance	200
Office Supplies	-
Rent	-
Salaries, Benefits & Wages	4,500
Telecommunication	-
Travel	50
Utilities	100
Bank Charges	50
Total Expenses	5,583
Earnings Before Interest & Taxes	**36,417**
Interest Expense	-
Earnings Before Taxes	**36,417**
Income Taxes	-
Net Earnings	**36,417**

Fundamental Accounting
Real-world Example to complete accounting cycle

5. Preparing the Balance Sheet

	Zoivu Logistic Co. Balance Sheet Mar. 31, 2020
Assets (USD)	
Current assets	
Cash	31,750
Bank	281,350
Accounts Receivable	-
Prepaid Expenses	1,000
Insurance Expense Adjusted	(83)
Inventory	-
Total current assets	314,017
Property	2,000,000
Equipment	5,000
Furniture & Fixture	3,000
Vehicle	35,000
Accumulated Depreciation	(600)
Goodwill	-
Total Assets (USD)	**2,356,417**
Liabilities (USD)	
Current Liabilities	
Accounts Payable	20,500
Accrued Expenses	-
Unearned Revenue	-
Total Current Liabilities	20,500
Long-term Debt	-
Other Long-term Liabilities	-
Total Liabilities (USD)	**20,500**
Shareholder's Equity	
Equity Capital	2,300,000
Retained Earnings	36,417
Owner's Withdrawal	(500)
Shareholder's Equity (USD)	**2,335,917**
Total Liabilities & Shareholder's Equity (USD)	**2,356,417**
Check	-

Fundamental Accounting

Real-world Example to complete accounting cycle

6. Preparing Statement of Cash Flows

Statement of cash flow is a very significant part of financial reporting, as this shows the **cash liquidity** in-and-out flow in your business. You constantly need cash to pay bills, new inventory purchases, fulfill purchase orders, taxes, and salaries. Thus, you as a business owner, manager, or for your business purpose, needs to understand your cash flow situation and that it can fluctuate between negative and positive depending on net earnings of the business.

Zoivu Logistic Co. Statement of Cash flow (USD) 31-Mar-20	
Operating Cash Flow	
Net Earnings	36,417
Plus: Depreciation & Amortization	600
Less: Changes in Working Capital	-
Cash from Operations	**37,017**
Investing Cash Flow	
Investments in Property & Equipment	43,000
Cash from Investing	**43,000**
Financing Cash Flow	
Issuance (repayment) of Debt	20,500
Issuance (repayment) of Equity	-
Cash from Financing	**20,500**
Net Increase (decrease) in Cash	14,517
Opening Cash Balance	300,000
Closing Cash Balance	**314,517**

The *"Closing Balance"* is the amount of cash available at Zoivu Co. at the end of March 2020, which is $314,517. This closing balance has been calculated by the opening balance of March. Thus, the closing balance of February has been calculated by adding total revenue deducted from total expenses

Fundamental Accounting

Real-world Example to complete accounting cycle

Closing the Account (Closing entry also known as closing the book)

Journal entries, which could be monthly or annually, will be made at the end of the accounting period for the purpose of transferring temporary accounts to permanent accounts.

Temporary vs. permanent accounts

- **Temporary accounts:** Accounts that supposed to be closed at the end of the accounting period. For example: All items in income statements, revenue, expense, gain and loss.

- **Permanent accounts:** Accounts that are transferrable from one accounting period to another and include all balance sheet items such as asset, liability, and equity. For example: AR, Inventory, AP, loan, retain earnings, and capital or owner's equity.

The main purpose of doing closing entries is to match the posted balance of retained earnings with reports on the statement of retained earnings. This also clears out all temporary accounts and starts with zero (0) new balance at the beginning of the next period (or when the income and expense accounts are restarted).

The Four Key Steps to close the books are as follows:

- **Revenue accounts closing**

The $24,000 generated from the income statement worked in the previous section.

Closing Income Account into Income Summary		
Mar 31, 2020	Debit	Credit
Service Sales/Income	42,000	
Income Summary		42,000
Total Debit & Credit	**42,000**	**42,000**

- **Expense accounts closing**

In order to do closing entry for expenses, we credit the expense accounts and Debit Income Summary to clear out or make them zero.

Fundamental Accounting

Real-world Example to complete accounting cycle

Closing Expense Accounts into Income Summary		
Mar 31, 2020	Debit	Credit
Income Summary	5,583	
Depreciation Expense		600
Gas Expense		50
Insurance Expense		83
Repair and Maintenance		200
Internet Charges		100
Bank Charges		50
Salary Expense		4,500
Total Debit & Credit	5,583	5,583

- *Income summary account closing (close the capital account)*

You can debit income summary and credit retained earnings in order to close the income summary account, where the total of $63,417 comes from the income statement report.

Close Income Summary Account		
Mar 31, 2020	Debit	Credit
Income Summary	36,417	
Retained earnings		36,417
Total Debit & Credit	36,417	36,417

- *Dividend account closing*

In this case, the entire Debit balance will be Credited and vice versa all Credit balance will be Debited with the title "Income Summary" on both sides

Close Dividends Summary Account		
Mar 31, 2020	Debit	Credit
Mr. Franklin Capital	500	
Mr. Franklin Drawing		500
Total Debit & Credit	500	500

PART (II)

QuickBooks Applications

GENERAL OVERVIEW ON QUICKBOOKS

Importance of Learning to Use QuickBooks

Versions of QuickBooks

New 2020 Features in QuickBooks

Difference between QuickBooks Desktop and QuickBooks Online

Setting Up and Creating a Company

Introduction: Homepage & Document Center

Setting Up Users with Different Access Permissions/Role/Password

Track Changes and User Entry in QB (Audit Log/Trail)

Creating a Standard Chart of Accounts, Printing, and Sharing

Backing Up QuickBooks Files Automatically and Regularly

Opening and Restoring Existing Company Files

Switching to Single-User Mode and Multi-Users Networking

Importing and Exporting QuickBooks Data with MS Excel Files

Closing the Book and Securing

Adding Priority to Do List and Reminders

Setting Up Your Employee List and Other Details

Managing Currencies, Setting Up Home Currency vs. Multiple Currencies

Entering and Tracking Vehicle Mileage

Preparing Letters with Envelopes

CREATING PRODUCT/SERVICES, DEPARTMENT/CLASSES (LISTS)

Adding items/categories of products/services list

Class list and business units/locations/projects

Adding Pricing List

Managing Sales Tax and Calculation

Discount Item List

EMPLOYEES/SUPPLIER LIST/VENDOR FOR MANAGING PAYABLES AND INVENTORY

Setting Up Your Employee List and Other Details

Vendor/Supplier Setup and Tracking Payables/Purchases on Credit

Setting Up Vendors(if 1099 Applies for Year-End Purposes)

Creating a Purchase Order (PO), Entering Bills, Paying Bills

Entering Bills for Payment and Reimbursement

Inventory Management

Managing Sales Tax

CREATING AND SETTING UP CUSTOMERS

Setup New Customer Account
Creating Estimates or Quotations

Creating Sales Orders

Creating Invoices and Sales Receipts (Selling on Cash/Credit)

Creating Statements and Assessing Financial Charges

Receiving Payments via Cash, Check, Debit, or E-Check against Invoice

Recording Refunds and Credits Refunded to Customer

Automatic Invoice Entry "Memories"

Adding Jobs and Applying Multiple Projects

Editing, Deleting, Active-Inactive, and Attaching Customer Documents

Customizing Your Invoice and Other Forms

Adding Logos and Customizing Invoices

BANKING AND RECONCILIATION

Making Journal Entries – Double Entry Bookkeeping

Searching Transactions and Info Faster (Invoice, Bill, PO)

REPORTING IN QUICKBOOKS

Company and Financial

Profit and Loss Standard

Profit and Loss Detail

Balance Sheet Standard Report

Customers and Receivable

Sales Reports

Vendors and Payables

Purchase Reports

Inventory Reports

Employees and Payroll

Banking Reports

Accountant and Taxes

List

HOMEPAGE

Company Snapshot

Category (I)

Category (II)

Category (III)

General overview on QuickBooks

Millions of small and medium-sized businesses, regardless of industries or business types, are using QuickBooks as an accounting software. A variety of editions were developed and introduced by Intuit in 1992. QuickBooks helps business owners and individuals manage income, expenses, production, cash flow, and keep track of customers and suppliers by automatically updating transactions and generating reports and other financial activities.

Scott Cook and Tom Proulx founded Intuit in 1983, only two years after IBM developed its personal computer. However, Quicken was the first product, and once QuickBooks launched in 1992, it became the most popular accounting software for small businesses.

Intuit launched QuickBooks Online in 2001. There are over 1.3 million international subscribers (3.2 million in the U.S.) to QuickBooks Online. There are over one million QuickBooks Self-Employed subscribers.

QuickBooks Enterprise launched in 2002 as a higher-end product, which claims to scale as many as 30 users and advanced inventory features.

Importance of Learning to Use QuickBooks

In today's world, numbers are crucial. They're the basis of logic that can help anyone make both personal and professional decisions. Thus, the more accurate information any individual or business entity has, the better

QuickBooks Applications

General overview on QuickBooks

decision they can make. Since QuickBooks is an accounting and financial management software for small and medium-sized businesses/owners, it's also very helpful to household financial management, planning, and budgeting.

Versions of QuickBooks

There are various versions of QuickBooks that business owners and households can use to manage their finance and accounting. They are the following:

- *QuickBooks Online*
- *QuickBooks Self-Employed*
- *QuickBooks Live Bookkeeping*
- *QuickBooks Desktop for Mac*
- *QuickBooks Desktop Pro*
- *QuickBooks Premier*
- *QuickBooks Enterprise*
- *QuickBooks Accountant*
- *QuickBooks Point of Sale*

New 2020 Features in QuickBooks

Every year, new features are added to QuickBooks. New, enhanced features in QuickBooks 2020 Pro, Premier, Accountant, and Enterprise are the following:

- *Combining multiple invoices into one e-mail*
- *Automating payment reminders to a customer*
- *Horizontally collapsing a column or expanding in reports (Job & Classes)*
- *Customer purchase order (PO) in email subject line*
- *Number in emails*
- *Company file search*
- *Smart help and access to live experts through messaging and call back options*
- *Easy upgrade*
- *Payroll status for Direct Deposit*

QuickBooks Applications

General overview on QuickBooks

Difference between QuickBooks Desktop and QuickBooks Online

QuickBooks Desktop is a one-time purchase that is installed on your personal computer (PC), whereas *QuickBooks Online* is a cloud-based subscription service that you can work from anywhere with an internet or Wi-Fi connection, at any time.

Setting Up and Creating a Company

The one secret in QuickBooks is that the better, accurate, and more detailed input you provide, the better output you receive. Thus, before starting to create your company file, steps need to be followed. In order to practice well, you can use the sample file that QuickBooks offered in the beginning, do some experiments, and test how it works.

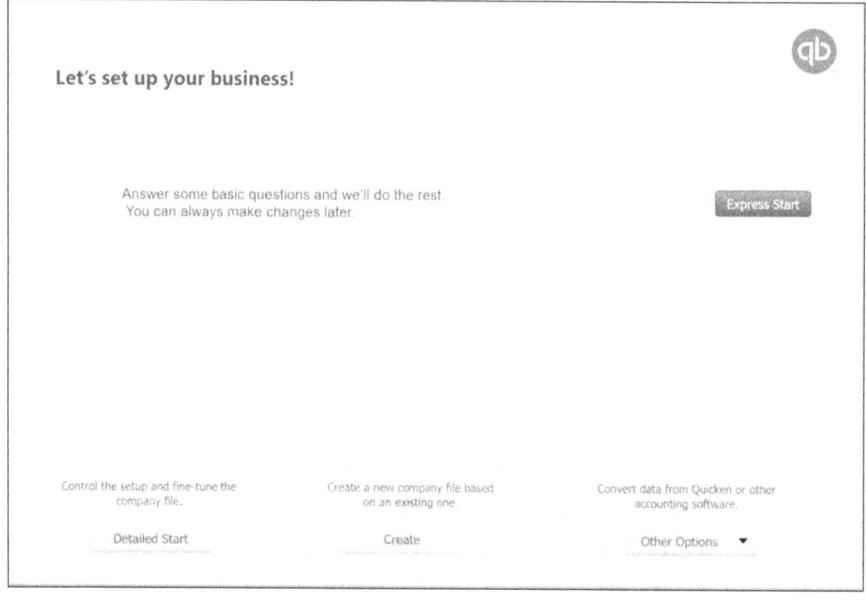

There are several options while creating company files from scratch:

- *Express Start:* The best choice to start creating a company file for the first time. QuickBooks helps navigate you through the process and will ask you more questions in each step before proceeding.

- *Detailed Start:* This is the best option if you're familiar with

QuickBooks Applications

General overview on QuickBooks

QuickBooks, since this method shortens the company file.

- Create and other options: This is best to use in case of opening an existing company file or converting existing records in another accounting program such as Quicken. With Express and Detailed Start, you're required to provide all basic information about your business/company to QuickBooks, such as contact information, tax ID, and location.

Introduction: Homepage & Document Center

QuickBooks desktop main homepage is a roadmap that allows you to work and do tasks while having access directly from this page. It shows a workflow of company transactional process including vendor, customers, employees, company, and banking activities.

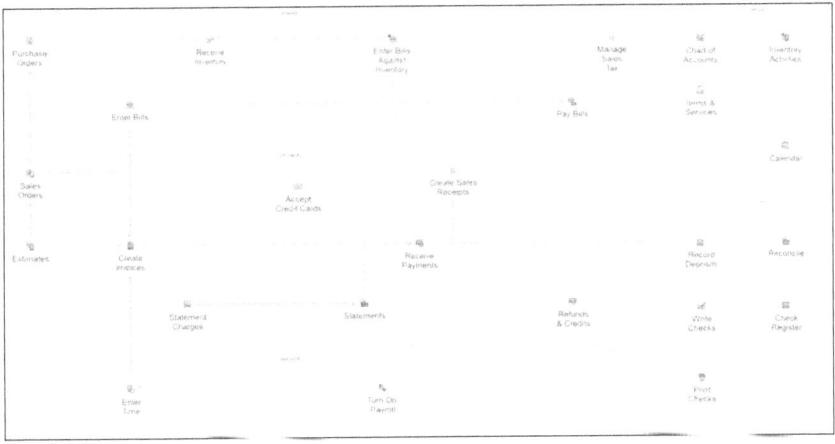

QuickBooks Applications

General overview on QuickBooks

We will discuss the homepage introduction and navigating QuickBooks in the following parts:

Part1: *Vendor area*

This is a shortcut for creating purchase orders, receiving inventory, entering Bills and Bills against inventory, and paying Bills.

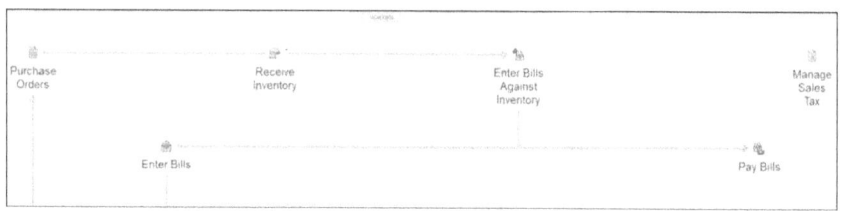

Part 2: *Customer Area*

If you understand the vendor area and workflow process, you will easily understand the customer area. It's a shortcut for creating sales orders, estimates, invoices, credit cards, sales or cash receipts, statement charges, statements, receiving payments, refunds, and credits that will save you valuable time in your homepage.

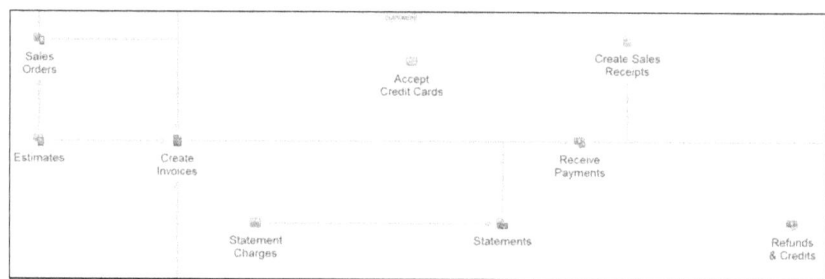

QuickBooks Applications

General overview on QuickBooks

Part 3: *Company and Banking Area*

As seen in the company section, these options are the fastest ways to create charts of the following: accounts, delete, active in active, adjust and edit, multicurrency, inventory activities, items, services, and calendar.

In the Banking section, you are provided with more facilities to record deposits, write cheques for paying bills, printing cheques, doing bank reconciliation, and checking registers. These options are like tasks you complete daily, which is why they are added to the QuickBooks homepage as "favorite" options for ease and efficiency.

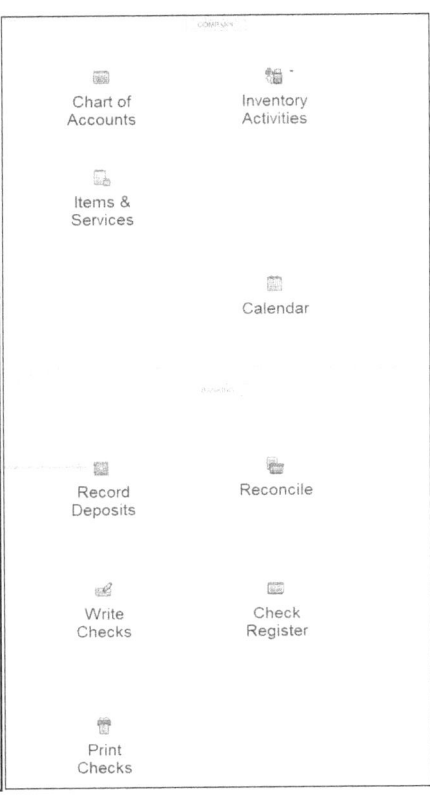

Setting Up Users with Different Access Permissions/Role/Password

Part 4: *Employees Area*

In this employee's section, you can enter and track times and turn on the payroll in QuickBooks.

QuickBooks Applications

General overview on QuickBooks

> Go to Homepage →Company

This is as simple as setting up a password on your personal computer or mobile device. Passwords need to be set up to protect your critical data, whether business or personal finances.

These are the following steps you should take:
- ➢ Determine who should be an admin user
- ➢ Go to: **Company→Setup users and password**
- ➢ On the user list window popup, choose **Admin→Edit and customize users for each role**
- ➢ Enter the admin name if applicable, or leave it as is and add different roles

Note: QuickBooks requires users to choose complex passwords at least seven letters or numbers, one special character (!$#*), and one uppercase letter (A-Z). **Password Ex:** *Quick123a*

As an admin, you can add different users and assign a password for each user. However, it depends on how many users your QuickBooks has, which typically starts from about 31 users based on each version of QuickBooks. For instance, if you're an admin working in the finance department, you can give permission to each department differently, accordingly to their working area.

For example, the following people are working at Zoivu Co.:
- Financial analyst
- Accountant
- Accounts payable
- Accounts receivable

QuickBooks Applications

General overview on QuickBooks

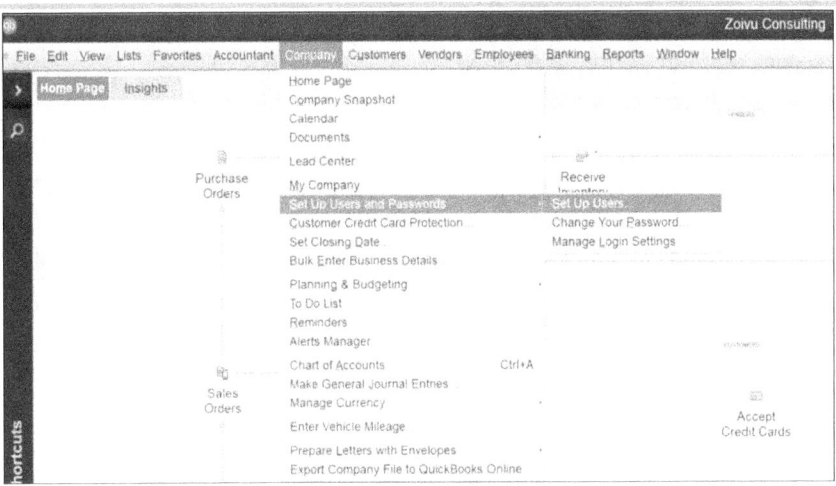

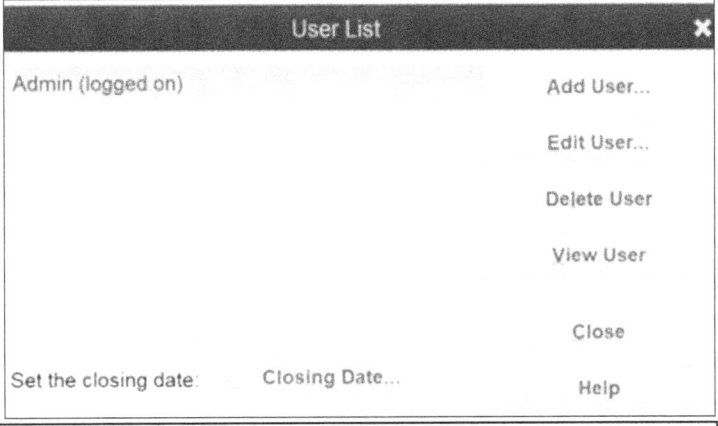

You can see that there is currently one user as an Admin on the left side, but you can create as many users as you want depending on capability of QuickBooks version and we created new user as an "Financial Analyst" in the next exhibit.

QuickBooks Applications

General overview on QuickBooks

In order to add a new account user, you need to make credentials (username and optional password), and then click "Next," as shown below.

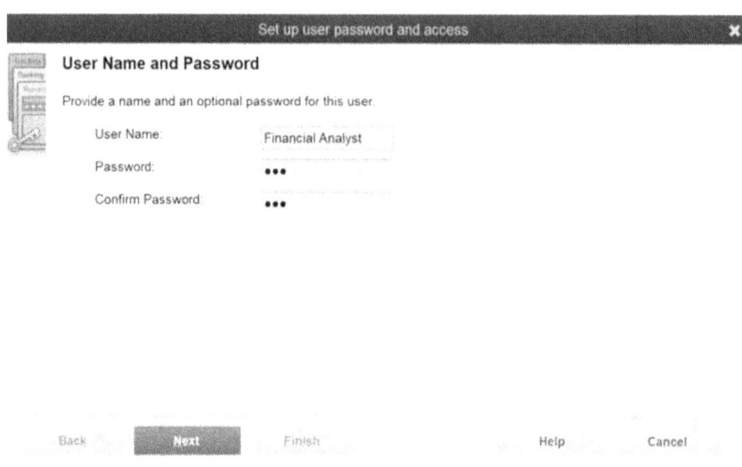

QuickBooks will then ask you to give access for the user you want as "Financial Analyst." You can simply customize this based on the area of work for that specific role, including all areas of QuickBooks or an external accountant

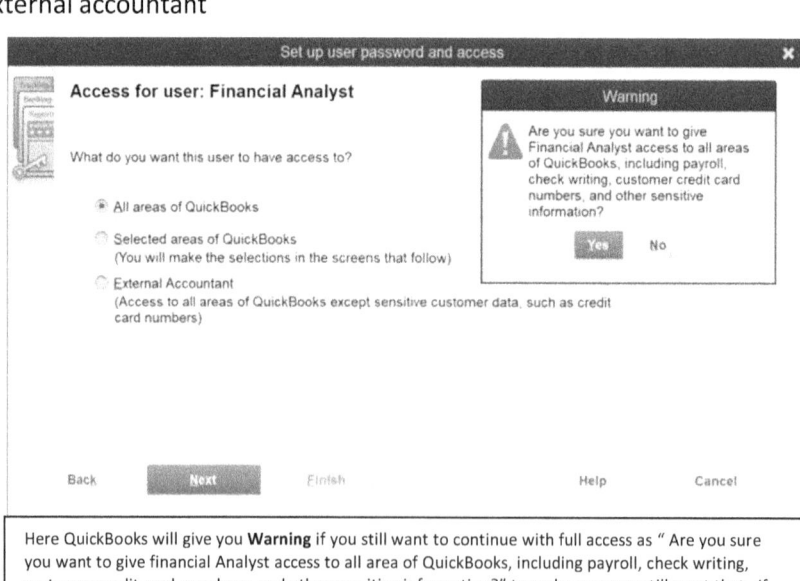

Here QuickBooks will give you **Warning** if you still want to continue with full access as " Are you sure you want to give financial Analyst access to all area of QuickBooks, including payroll, check writing, customer credit card, numbers, and other sensitive information?" to make sure you still want that. If right, then click Yes to continue for the next step. Then you will see a checklist that what are this role will have access.

QuickBooks Applications

General overview on QuickBooks

As you see above, the user "**Financial Analyst**" needs all access to QuickBooks. To avoid further questions or confusion, we can give access to all areas of QuickBooks and then customize this later.

This new user has been added in the following exhibit:

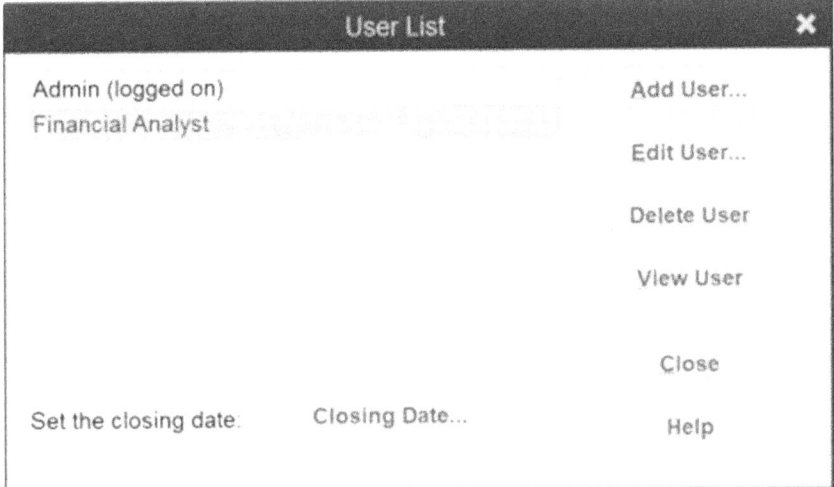

Track Changes and User Entry in QB (Audit Log/Trail)

This is an interesting feature that allows an admin user who makes an entry to change, delete, or edit in/from QuickBooks. In order to have access to this, do the following steps to get Audit/Trail report:

- From Homepage Menu → Reports
- Accountant and Taxes
- Click on "Audit Trail"
- Select all or custom for any specific period

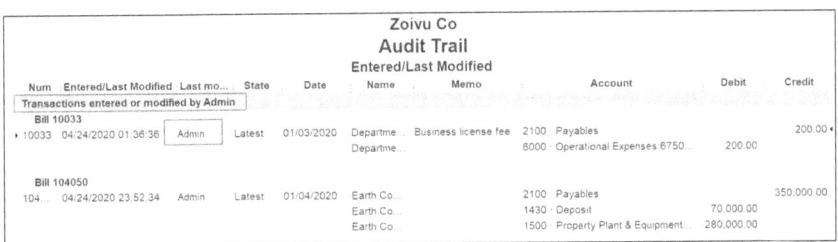

QuickBooks Applications

General overview on QuickBooks

Creating a Standard Chart of Accounts, Printing, and Sharing

There are five main categories for the standard chart of accounts (COA) that are used to keep track of financial transactions. However, these not limited, as there are hundreds of other sub-accounts to the main accounts, such as:

- Asset
- Liability
- Capital or Shareholder's Equity
- Revenue
- Expense

A sample of this chart of the account listed is in Appendix (A) for your review. There are different ways to access the chart of account. Use the following steps:

- Hold down the keys Ctr+ A
- Go to List in the home menu bar
- Go to the company→Accountant (if you're using QuickBooks Premiere 2020).

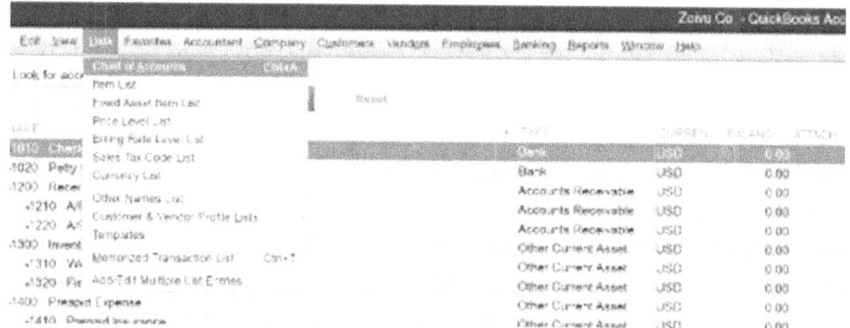

The Chart of Accounts contains the name, which is a list of all five accounts, type of accounts, currencies, Balance total, and attachment needed for any supporting documentation related to COA.

QuickBooks Applications

General overview on QuickBooks

In order to create, edit or edit an account, you can press any of the below combination of keys:

- Create: CTRL+N
- Edit: CTRL+E
- Delete: CTRL+D

You can also follow the instructions (as shown below) by clicking on the account located in the bottom left corner of the chart of the account page. Then click either **New**, **Edit Account**, or **Delete Account**, respectively.

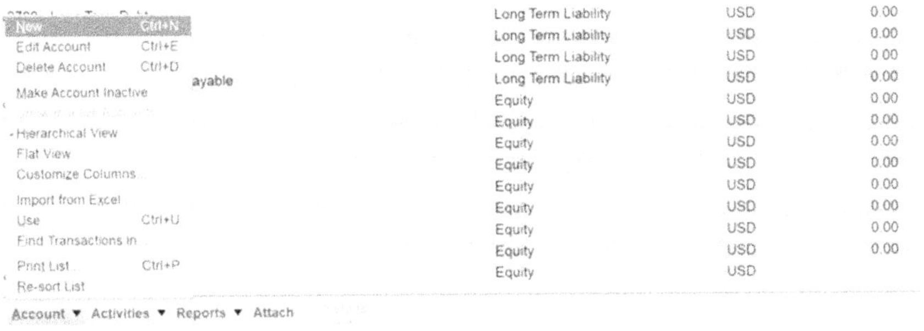

QuickBooks Applications

General overview on QuickBooks

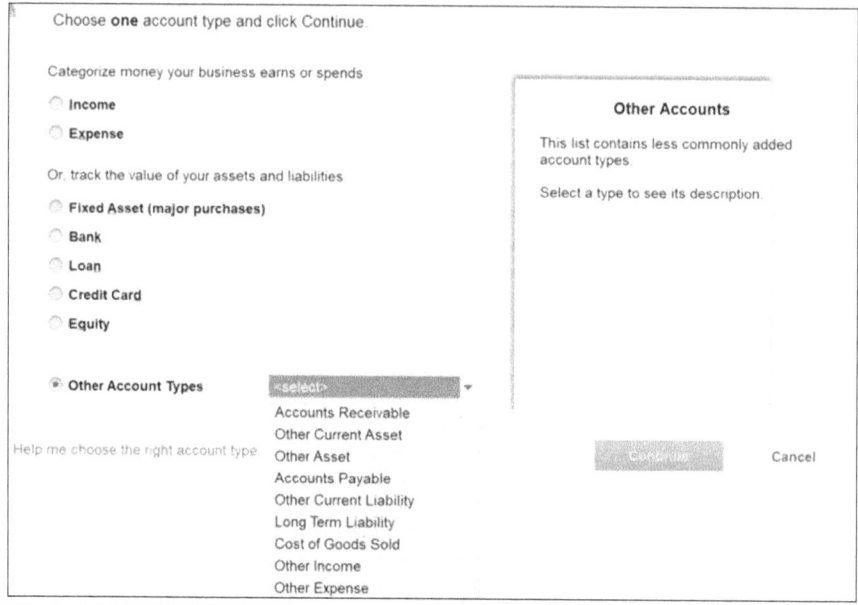

After you click "New," the next page will pop up that allows you to choose one account type. Click to continue and select the right account in order to categorize money your company earns or spends as the income and expense or to track the value of your assets and liabilities.

However, there are other list of accounts under "**Other Account Types**" that you can choose based upon the account you want to create.

Backing Up QuickBooks Files Automatically and Regularly

Before beginning to make a backup for your company QuickBooks file, let's discuss its advantages. You can create a backup either locally or online.

Local backups save your company file locally to a removable storage device such as a CD, USB flash drive, or any folder in your network. However, getting automatic online backup saves your company QuickBooks data and significant documents through Intuit's online backup solution. Remember that fees may apply to this online backup option.

QuickBooks Applications

General overview on QuickBooks

The following steps are necessary to create a copy of your QB file as a local backup:

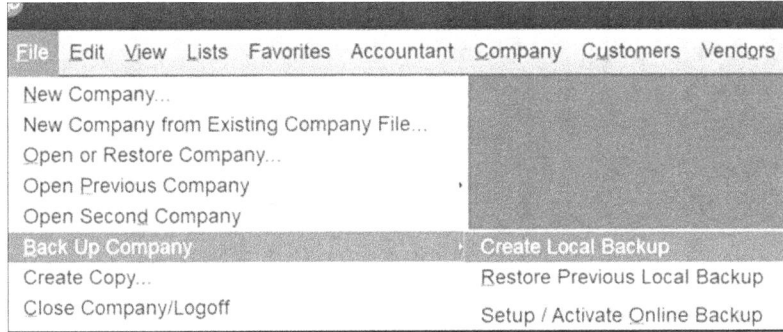

- Login to QB. If using multi-user mode, change it back to **single-user mode**.
- Go to the **File** menu and choose **Backup Company** (as shown above).
- Choose **Local Backup** (as shown above) and select **Local Backup→Next**.
- Select the folder location in which you wish to store your backup file (i.e. Drive (C).

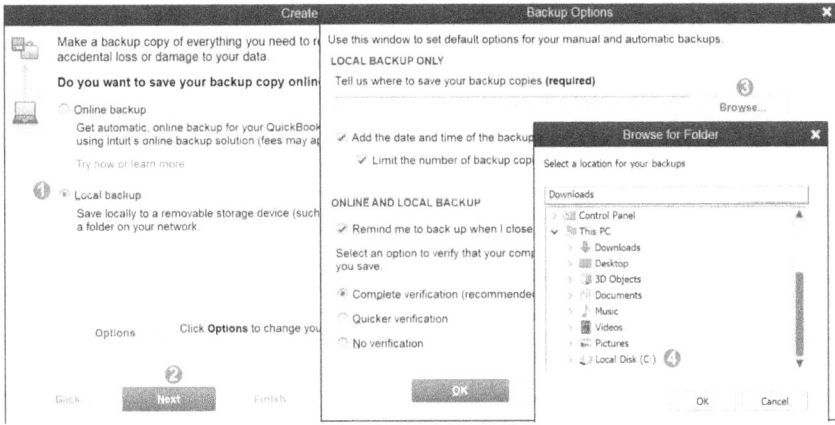

QuickBooks Applications

General overview on QuickBooks

Opening and Restoring Existing Company Files

QuickBooks can always restore a company file to get back to your previous data backup file. For instance: You made a backup on Jan. 1, 2020. You can bring back the QuickBooks file to that same point in time if you wish, depending on your situation.

Sometimes QuickBooks gives an error message while opening a previous backup file, so you can use these troubleshooting methods:

How to Restore a File or Open a Previous Backup File:

- ➢ Open QuickBooks
- ➢ Select the **File** menu, then **Open** or **Restore company file**
- ➢ Restore the file based on its type and where you saved it (i.e. local backup or online backup)

• From a company file (see images below for visual steps):
  - ➢ Select a company file → select **Next**.
  - ➢ Open the appropriate folder→ choose the company file.
  - ➢ Select **Open**→Enter your password.

QuickBooks Applications

General overview on QuickBooks

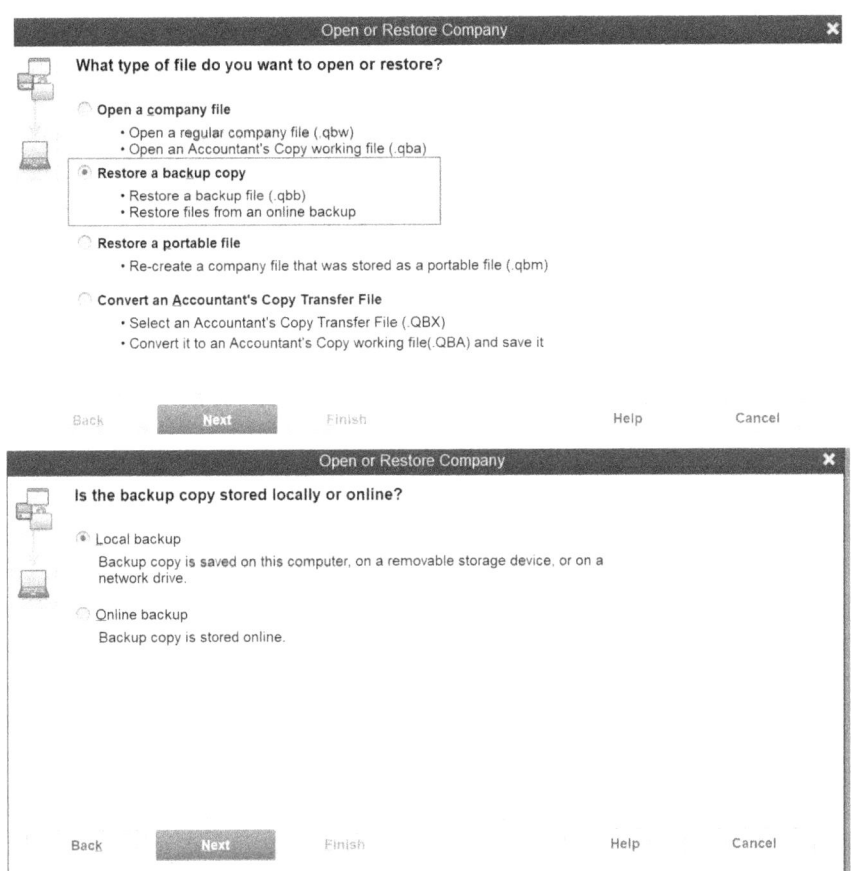

Switching to Single-User Mode and Multi-Users Networking

In order to change and switch to multi-user mode or single-user mode, simply go to the **File** menu and click on "**Switch multi-user mode/single-user mode**," depending upon on the current status.

QuickBooks Applications

General overview on QuickBooks

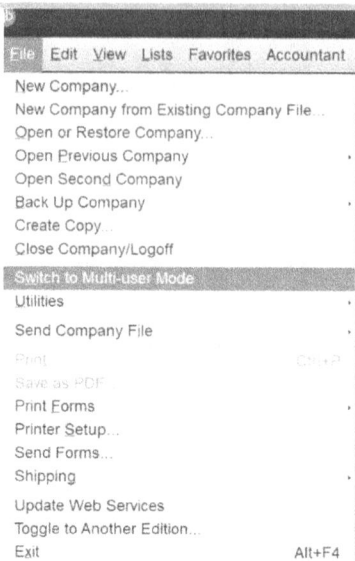

Single-user mode limits access to your QuickBooks company file to one person at a time. However, if you decide to use QuickBooks for multiple people, you need to change the mode from single to multiple (and vice versa). QuickBooks will message about this action if you're doing anything without changing this option.

With more than one user license, you can switch to multiple-user mode, where you can log in at a company file on different computers and/or locations. You would be able to work and edit while others are working on QB at the same time.

For example: If you're working for a company that you're using as an Admin in QuickBooks, you can email or message everyone that you are changing from single to multiple user mode to ensure that everyone in the office is in the loop.

Importing and Exporting QuickBooks Data with MS Excel Files

QuickBooks allows you to import and export different lists and transaction types using various formats. For instance:

- Importing Excel files: You can import customer, vendor, items, and chart of accounts from Excel with the following options:
    - Standard import
    - Advance import
    - Add/edit multiple lists
- Exporting Excel files: You can export customer, vendor, payroll

QuickBooks Applications

General overview on QuickBooks

lists, and transactions into an Excel file, which can later be customized:
- Customer/Vendor/Payroll List and Transactions
- Items
- Reports

- **Chat or communicate between co-workers (QuickBooks Messenger):** This feature is only available if you're using QuickBooks in multi-user mode, which enables you to chat between co-workers and other company users in QuickBooks. It also enables you to log out other users when you want to switch QuickBooks from single-user mode to multi-user mode. To have access to this feature, you can:
    - Go to the Company file and click on the option "Chat with a Co-worker."

Closing the Book and Securing

Luckily, QuickBooks desktop creates an automatic adjustment in preparation for the coming year, so you do not need to worry about closing the book. Here is how QuickBooks performs the year-end adjustment:

- QuickBooks automatically adjusts your income and expense account into zero (0) at year-end. This allows you to start your new fiscal year with zero net profit.

- Example of adjustment entry QuickBooks makes: If your profit for the year was $5,000, the equity section in your balance sheet would show a line for a net income of $5,000 on the last day of your fiscal year.

- QuickBooks will increase your "retained earnings" equity account on the first day of the new fiscal year by the prior year's net profit of (EX: $5,000) and decrease your net income by the same amount so you can begin each new fiscal year with zero net income.

Note: Closing entries are usually made by the end of the fiscal year in order to transfer income and expense balances to retained earnings and zero out these accounts. The closing should happen after all adjustment

QuickBooks Applications

General overview on QuickBooks

entries are made, which helps once the books are closed. No entry should be made in the closed period (month/year).

For more information on how to restrict the account once it is closed, see the following steps:

> QuickBooks Homepage →**Company**
> Set Closing Date
> Accounting
> Company preferences
> Closing date → Set Date/Password
> Customize at your preference

Step one

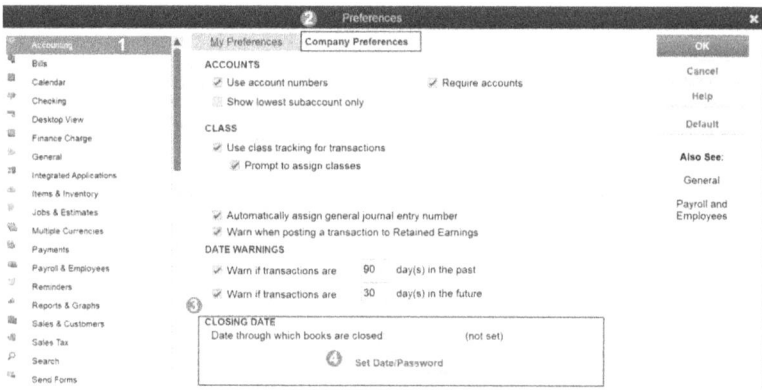

Step two

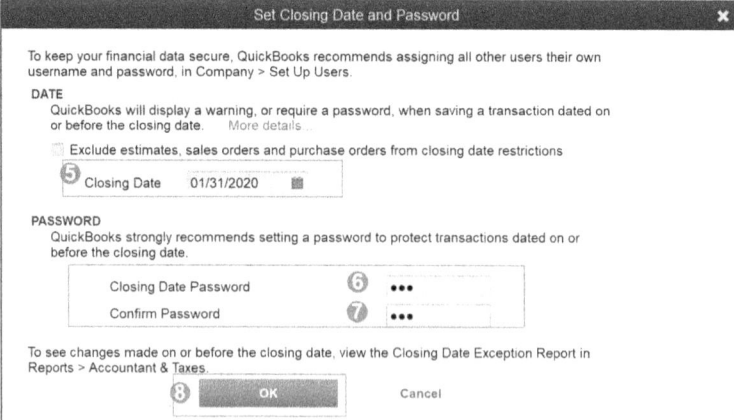

QuickBooks Applications

General overview on QuickBooks

Adding Priority to Do List and Reminders

A *"to do list"* prompts you with reminders before the deadline of when different tasks need to be done, such as paying taxes, paying bills, processing payroll on time, etc. If you want to delete the reminder and no longer receive alerts, you can click on the trash can icon.

You can add multi-reminders for each task by following the steps below:

> ➤ From QuickBooks, go to the homepage menu bar and select >**Edit**
>
> ➤ Select **Preferences**
>
> ➤ Click on **Company Preferences**
>
> ➤ You can choose your desired option >**Reminders** and then click "**OK**"

Managing Currencies, Setting Up Home Currency vs. Multiple Currencies

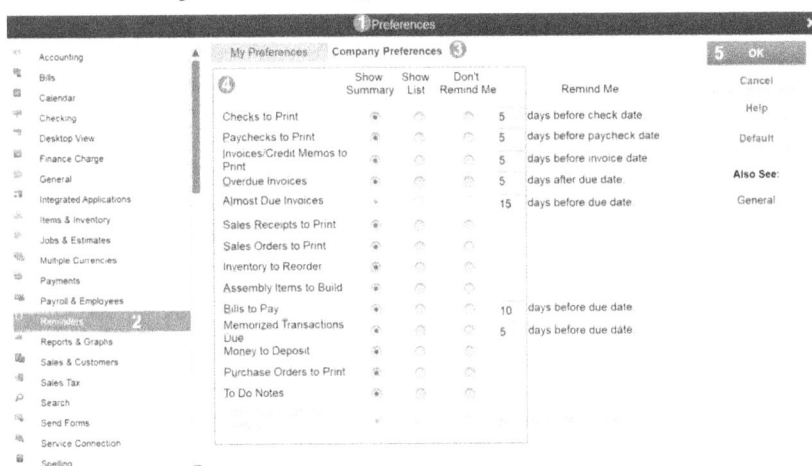

If you have operations in more than in one country or overseas, you will use multicurrency in your daily transactions or for reporting and tax purposes. QuickBooks allows you to track foreign currencies. With this feature, you can assign a specific currency type on the accounts, such as customers, vendors, price levels, bank accounts, credit card accounts, account receivables, and payables.

It's very important to remember while you're creating a chart of

QuickBooks Applications

General overview on QuickBooks

accounts for the first time, you have the option to select your home currency or main currency when you start preparing reports.

■ *Turning on Multicurrency and Setting Up Home Currency*

> ➢ From the homepage, go to→**Edit Menu** and then **Preferences**
> ➢ Choose **Multiple Currencies**
> ➢ **Company Preferences**→ click "**Yes, I use more than one currency**."
> ➢ From the drop-down menu, click on **Home Currency**

For example, let's add **Euro** as another currency in QuickBooks.

> ➢ From the homepage, go to **Company**→**Manage Currency**
> ➢ Currency list
> ➢ Find "Euro" and then Un-tick the "X" to activate
> ➢ From the homepage, go to **Edit**→**Company Preferences**→**Multiple Currencies**

- In order to do transactions with various currencies, you need to **add foreign currency accounts first** because you can only assign one currency for each individual account. While you are creating a new account, you can select which currency you set up in relation to each customer or vendor.

- You can also update exchange rates by downloading **Exchange Rates** if your home currency is in USD. The following steps navigate you to download exchange rates:

> ➢ From the homepage, click List → select the Currency List
> ➢ Activities→Download Latest Exchange Rates (shown below).

QuickBooks Applications

General overview on QuickBooks

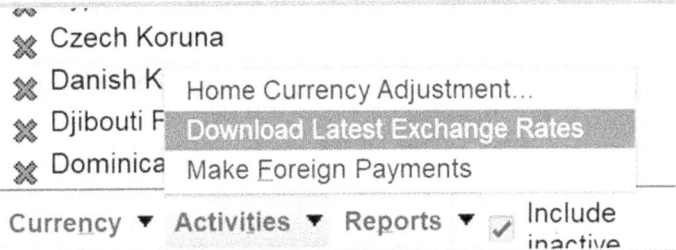

Enter and Track Vehicle Mileage

Tracking vehicle mileage is a feature in QuickBooks Desktop that allows you to track your business miles and enter expenses accordingly. In order to track VM, follow these steps:

- From the homepage menu, go to Company→Select Company →Enter Vehicle Mileage

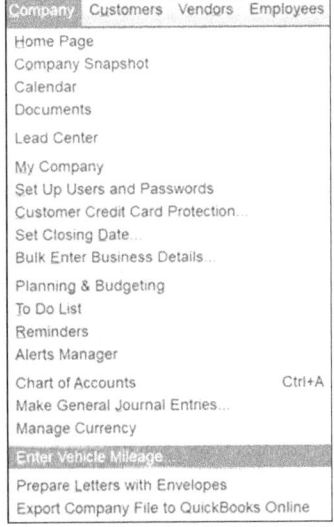

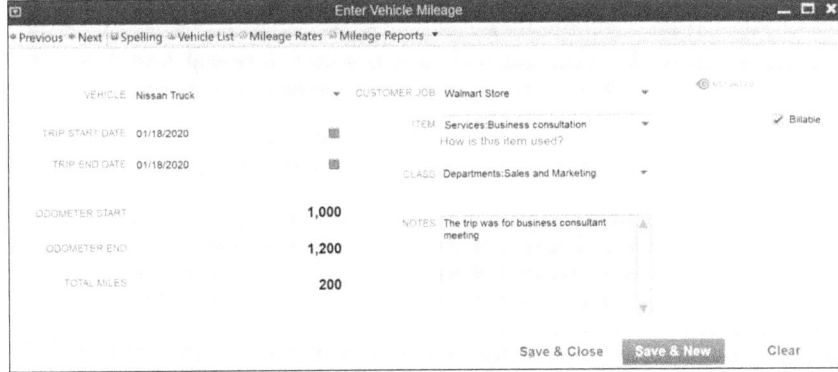

QuickBooks Applications

General overview on QuickBooks

▪ Preparing Letters with Envelopes

There is a wide variety of business envelopes and templates in QuickBooks. You can download, customize, and apply all of these formats in your daily operations.

▪ *Use the following steps to prepare envelopes:*

- Go to Homepage→**Company**
- Select Prepare **Letters with Envelopes**
- From the Open window, select **Recipients**
- Choose **Select Template**
- Customize or **Edit Letter Template**
- View or Edit an Existing Letter Template
- Click **Next**
- Save file (File→Save As)
- Use the **new letter template**

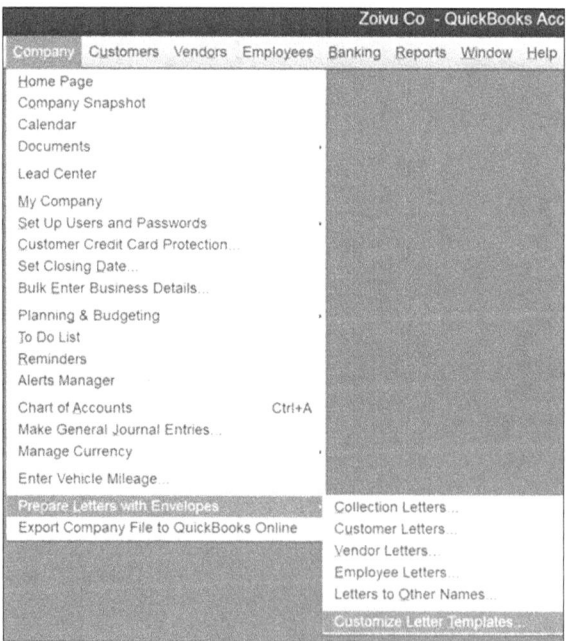

QuickBooks Applications

General overview on QuickBooks

Example: If you wish to download a birthday letter for your employee, select **Employee** (under Types of Letters) →**Employee Birthday** →**Next**

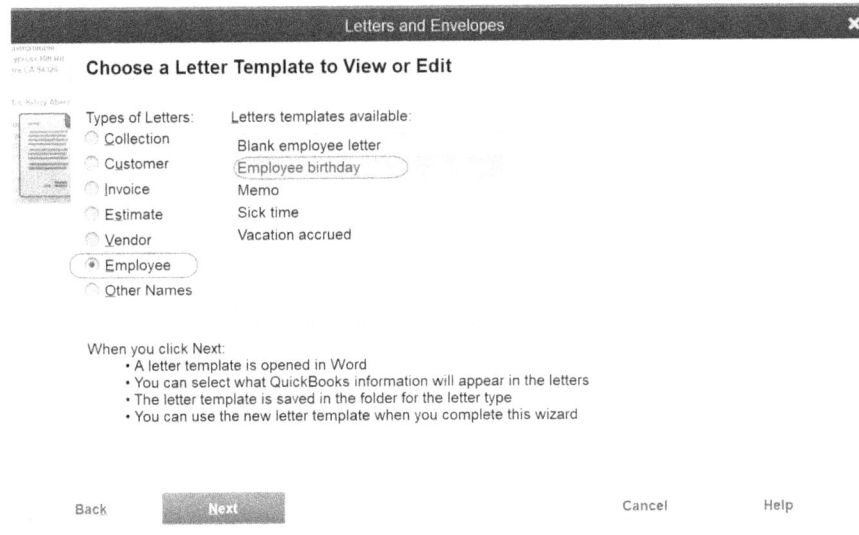

Creating Products/Services, Departments/Classes (Lists)

Adding items/categories of products/services list

Lists are the blocks for the wall. You can create and customize almost anything as tools in QuickBooks. You can even apply them to make transactions easier and more efficient.

Some examples of these include a chart of account list, item list, fixed asset list, price level list, billing rate level list, sales tax code list, currency list, other names list, customer and vendor profile lists, business forms, and templates list.

You can go to the Homepage and click **Lists**, as shown below:

QuickBooks Applications

Creating Products/services, department/classes (Lists)

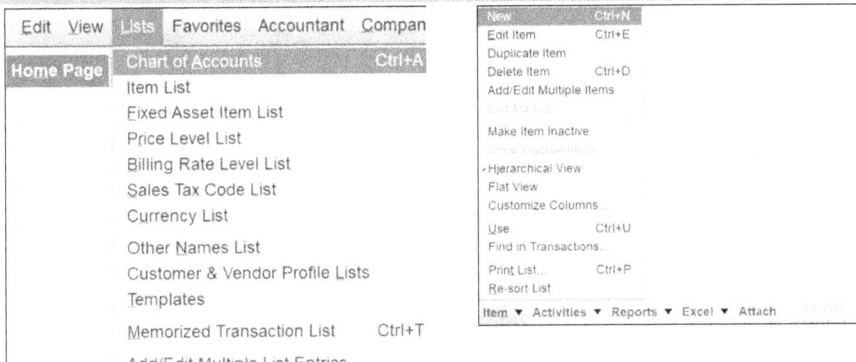

Here, you will learn how each type of list works.

Item list: There are different types of lists in this category that allow you to create products and services, track inventory, taxes, etc.

- There is no "Class List" under the list
- In order to add the class list, go to the homepage and follow the next steps:
    a) Edit
    b) Preferences
    c) Accounting
    d) Company preferences
    e) Class

QuickBooks Applications
Creating Products/services, department/classes (Lists)

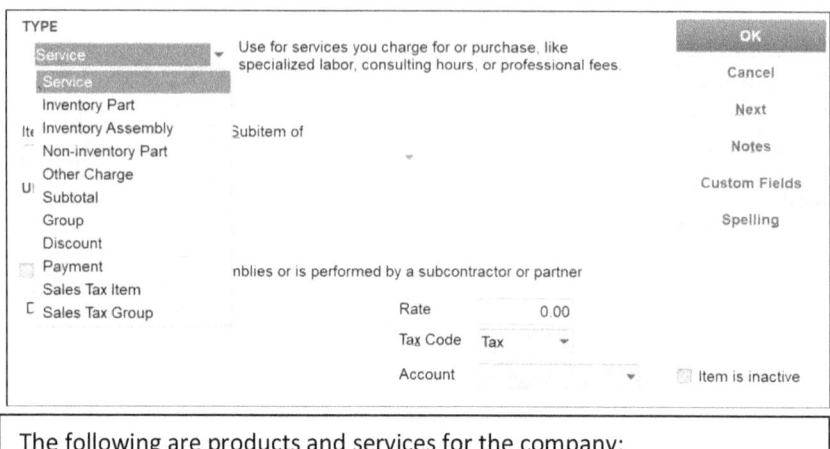

The following are products and services for the company:

Product:
- a) Pen
- b) Notebook
- c) Flipchart
- d) Training manual

Services:
- a) Finance workshop tax
- b) QuickBooks workshop
- c) Business consultation

Class List and Business Units/Locations/Projects

How to Activate a Class List

There are a few ways to customize or add a Class List from the "Preferences" section under "Edit" from the homepage menu. We add Class Lists to classify expenses or revenue into specific departments or classes.

QuickBooks Applications
Creating Products/services, department/classes (Lists)

In order to add the class list, go to the home page and proceed with the following steps:

- Edit
- Preferences
- Accounting
- Company Preferences
- Class
- Tick "Use class tracking for transaction"
- Click Ok

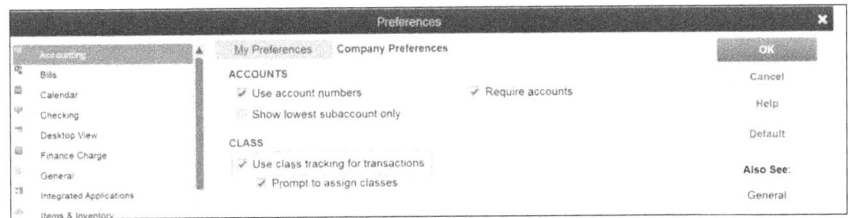

If you go to the list and the class has already appeared, you can compare the outcomes with the images below:

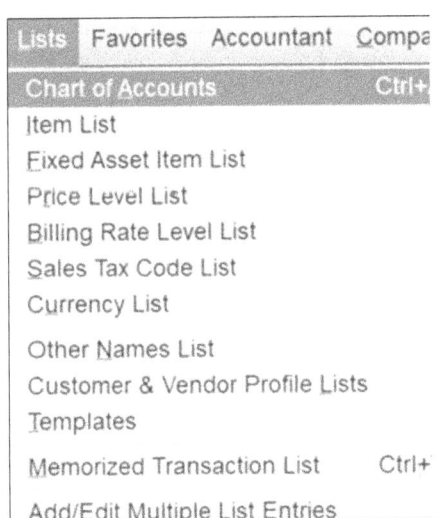
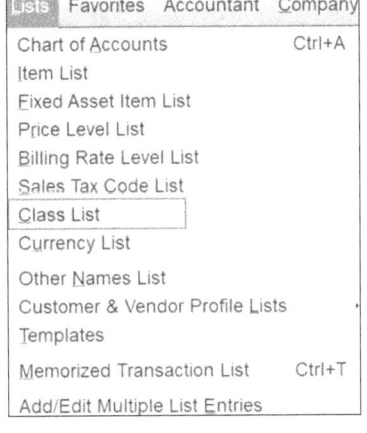

QuickBooks Applications

Creating Products/services, department/classes (Lists)

Let's begin understanding why class is important in the real-world. For instance, Zoivu Co. has some departments that generate revenue and have expenses to be charged individually. At the end of the month, you can get a report of sales, expense, and profit and loss by class under the report section. The following are the current departments:

- Finance and Accounting
- Human Resources
- Production
- Sales and Marketing
- Procurement

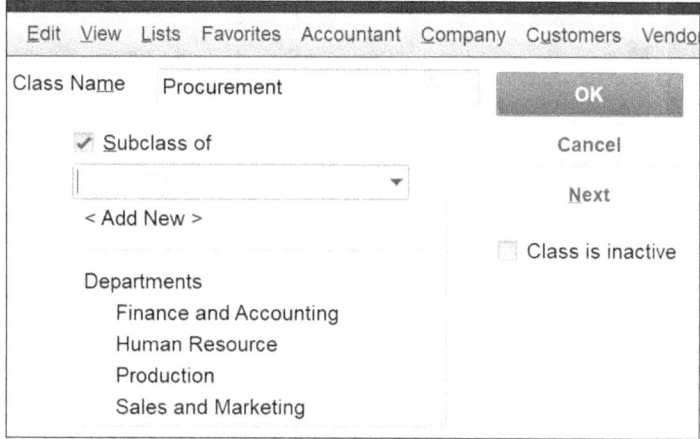

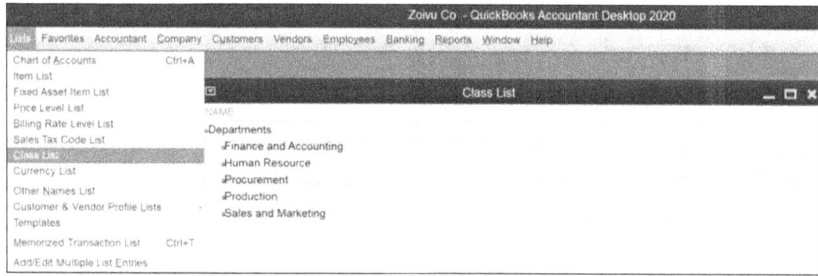

QuickBooks Applications

Creating Products/services, department/classes (Lists)

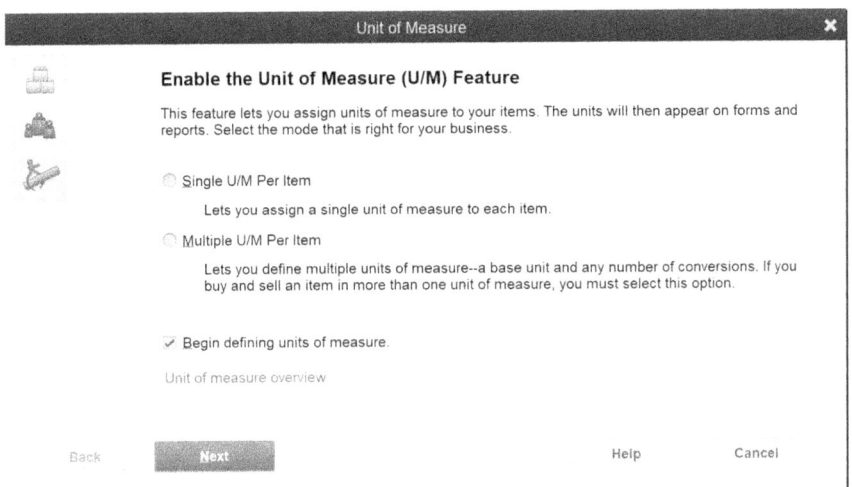

TYPE			OK
Service	▼	Use for services you charge for or purchase, like specialized labor, consulting hours, or professional fees.	Cancel
			Next
Item Name/Number	☐ Subitem of		Notes
Finance workshop tax		▼	Custom Fields
UNIT OF MEASURE			Spelling
Enable...			
☐ This service is used in assemblies or is performed by a subcontractor or partner			
Description		Rate	0.00
Finance workshop tax		Tax Code	Tax ▼
		Account	▼ ☐ Item is inactive

QuickBooks Applications
Creating Products/services, department/classes (Lists)

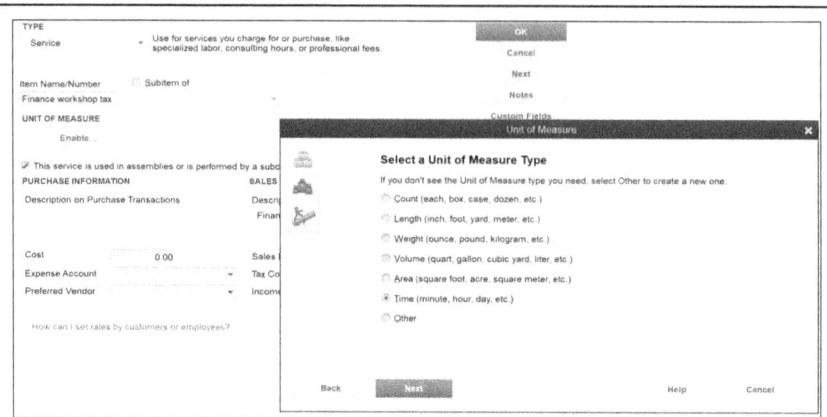

Here is what it looks like after completing a three-item list to produce something like a flipchart, notebook, and pen. You can use sub-accounts to show in each respective category, as shown below.

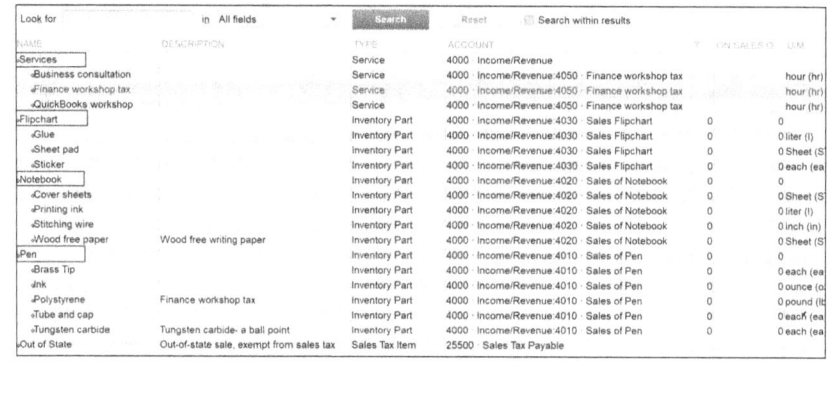

QuickBooks Applications
Creating Products/services, department/classes (Lists)

Adding Pricing Lists

Depending on what version of QuickBooks you use, adding prices or pricing level is a feature that allows you to charge a different price to customers. If there is fluctuation in the market in price (whether it changes daily, weekly, or by any percentage), you can manipulate the sales prices of all the products/items you sell individually by item or a fixed percentage(%).

To have access to Price Lists, go to the homepage →List→Price Level List

For instance, Zoivu Co. decided to add a 2% promotional discount to all the items below.

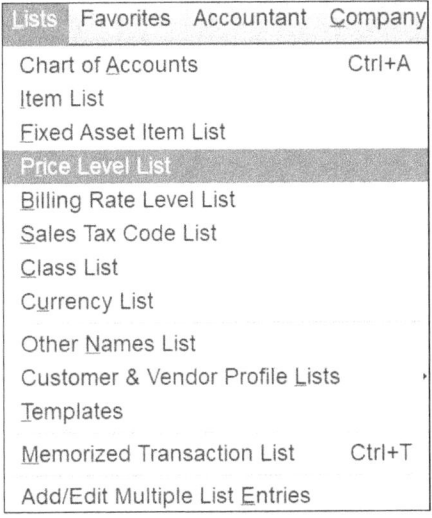

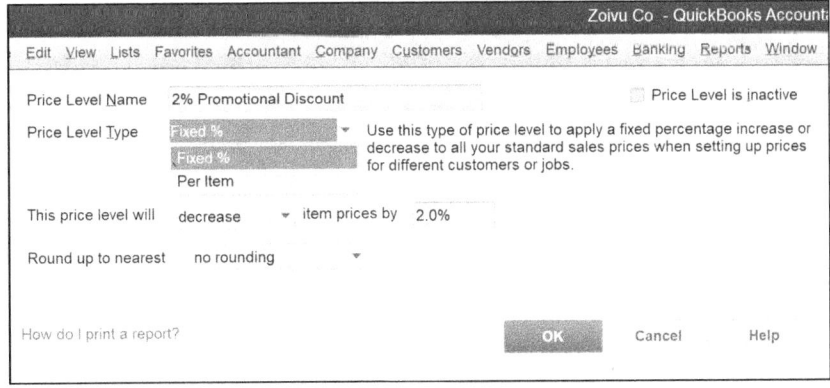

QuickBooks Applications
Creating Products/services, department/classes (Lists)

■ Managing Sales Tax and Calculation

Since you are required to collect taxes for certain goods and services, you may already know how to calculate tax as a business owner or freelancer. QuickBooks will assist you with keeping an accurate record of these taxes so you can monitor and remit them to the appropriate tax-collecting agency depending on the area you are located.

■ *How to Record Sales Tax in QuickBooks*

- ➤ From the homepage, go to → **Edit** → **Preferences**
- ➤ Choose **Sales Tax→Company Preferences**
- ➤ Select "**Yes**" (this turns the option on)
- ➤ Select and customize "**Sales Tax Item**"
- ➤ Assign sales tax code
- ➤ Set up sales tax with accrual or on a cash basis
- ➤ Setup timing structure: Monthly, Quarterly, or Annually
- ➤ Click "**OK**" to process

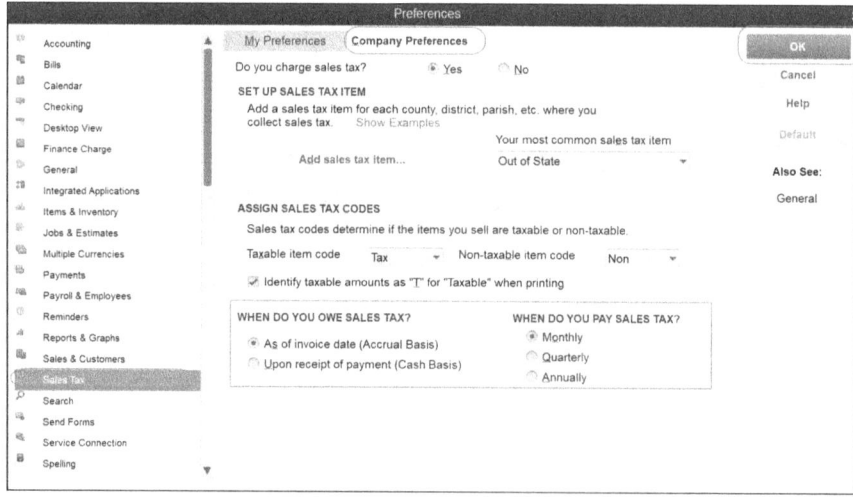

QuickBooks Applications
Creating Products/services, department/classes (Lists)

Discount Item List

When you wish to give a discount to customers on an invoice or an estimate, you need to create a "**Discount Item List**" before you apply it. Use the following steps as a guideline:

- QuickBooks homepage menu →**Item List**
- Right click anywhere, choose **New**(or click on left side corner as "**Item**")
- Select type on the drop-down as **Discount**
- Enter the **Item Name/Number** and **Description**
- **Amount or %**(or leave it blank in case of applying different amount/percentage)
- From the **Account**(drop-down menu), select the income account you wish to track (the discount given to customers)
- Select appropriate **Tax Code** and then click "**OK**"
- **Save** and close

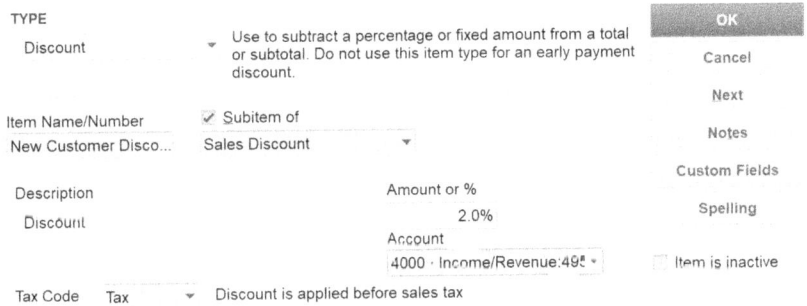

Employees/Supplier List/Vendors For Managing Payables And Inventory

Setting Up Your Employee List and Other Details

As mentioned earlier, the best tip to learn about dealing with data in QuickBooks is the following: the more accurate "Input," the better and more reliable "Output" you will get.

The same applies here as the employee center, vendor center, and customer center. To add a new employee or to modify their information, you can enter the following information:

- *Personal: Name* and social security number (other fields are optional)
- *Contact or Address:* Home address of the employee, cellphone, email or fax, and other additional information (optional)
- *Employment Details:* Enter their hire date, leave of absence and resignation or termination. If you enter the release date, you need to remove it before you're able to pay staff.

The advantage of entering your employees in QuickBooks is that it helps you organize and centralize all their information in one place.

You can always adjust and customize based on the type of employment, such as seasonal, tax-exempt, or even working visas.

QuickBooks Applications
Employees supplier/list/vendors for managing payables and inventory

Let's begin with an example of Zoivu Co.'s CFO. His name appeared as John Abc.

Step One:

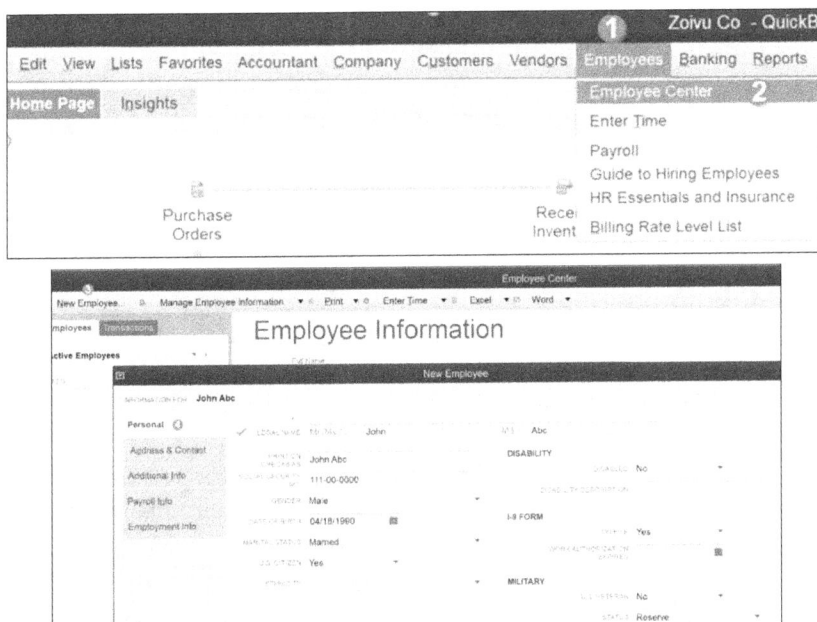

Step Two

The following steps need to be considered in order to enter each individual employee successfully in QuickBooks:

- ➢ In QuickBooks homepage, go to **Employees** and then select the **Employee Center**.
- ➢ Choose **New Employee** and enter their information as needed and optional.
- ➢ Click on the **Personal** tab and complete all fields.
- ➢ Click on **Address** and **Contact**.
- ➢ Click on the **Additional Information**. If you'd like to add extra info, use the **Custom Field**.
- ➢ Click **Payroll Info** and enter **Compensation and Benefits**(if eligible).

QuickBooks Applications
Employees supplier/list/vendors for managing payables and inventory

> Select **Employment Info** and complete. When done, hit "OK."

Step Three

After all fields have been completed and entered, you will see the result as the following form. The number of new employees you created will be listed under "John Abc" sequentially, as shown below.

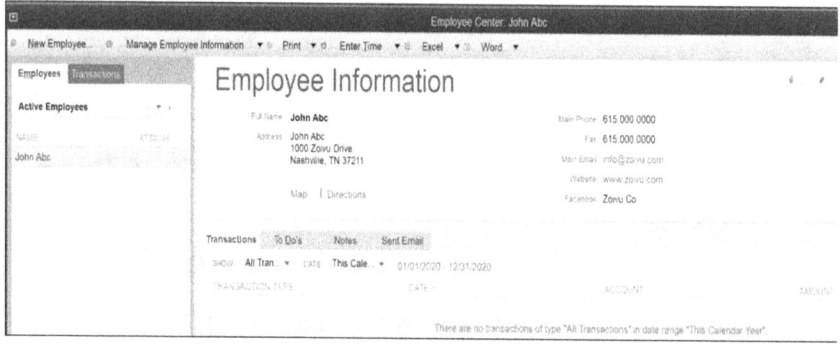

Payroll is a separate section in QuickBooks that manages timing, deduction, compensation, and more related to employees. In large companies, there is a specific department that handles payroll. Once you have decided to activate Payroll, the first step is to add employees and other details.

Follow the steps below to set up employees in Payroll:

> Choose **Employees** from the left-hand menu, and then click **Add Employee**

> Enter **employee personal details** and click **next**

> Enter the **employee details** (start date, pay rate, etc.)

> Enter the **Bank** details and type of account

> Click the **next** button

> Input the **tax file declaration detail**

> Your employee can now be included in payment runs. Further details can always be added later.

QuickBooks Applications
Employees supplier/list/vendors for managing payables and inventory

Vendor/Supplier Setup and Tracking Payables/Purchases on Credit

You only need to set up a vendor account if you need to purchase either in cash or credit. If the purchase is made on credit, there would be payment terms. For instance: Net 15, 30, or 60 days. In short, a vendor is a person or entity who sells a service or product, and business makes purchases form.

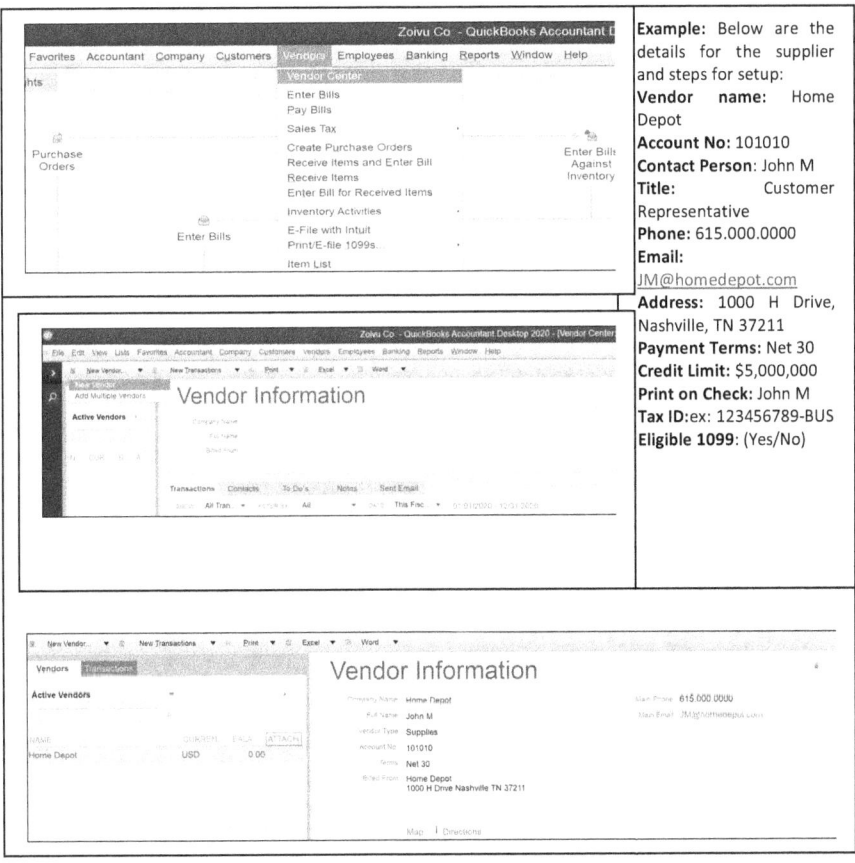

Example: Below are the details for the supplier and steps for setup:
Vendor name: Home Depot
Account No: 101010
Contact Person: John M
Title: Customer Representative
Phone: 615.000.0000
Email: JM@homedepot.com
Address: 1000 H Drive, Nashville, TN 37211
Payment Terms: Net 30
Credit Limit: $5,000,000
Print on Check: John M
Tax ID: ex: 123456789-BUS
Eligible 1099: (Yes/No)

QuickBooks Applications
Employees supplier/list/vendors for managing payables and inventory

Setting Up Vendors (if 1099 Applies for Year-End Purposes)

Use Federal 1099 tax forms to report payments of $600 or more to non-employees or unincorporated businesses. If you paid a vendor more than $600 in a year, you need to fill out a 1099-MISC form. When setting up a vendor account, it's important to select eligibility for 1099 by selecting (Yes/No).

To get a report on how many vendors are eligible for 1099 and print it at the end of the year, follow these steps:

- Go to Report(or Vendor tab)
- Vendors and Payables
- Select 1099 Summary or 1099 Details
- Print E-file 1099s

    - 1099 Wizard
    - Review 1099 Vendors
    - 1099 Summary Report
    - 1099 Detail Report
    - Order 1099 Form

Creating a Purchase Order (PO), Entering Bills, Paying Bills

Creating a purchase order (PO):

A purchase order is a business contract that works as an offer to purchase goods issued by a buyer to a seller containing details such as product, quantity, price, and term of payment or method of shipping. This is an optional way of the procurement process, and some small companies do not prefer to process "POs."

Use the following steps to create a purchase order:

- Go to the **Vendor** tab
- Scroll down and select **Create Purchase Orders**
- Select **Vendor Name**

QuickBooks Applications
Employees supplier/list/vendors for managing payables and inventory

- Select **Class** if you purchase for any specific department (optional)
- Fill out **date** and **PO Number** and **Shipping Address**
- Fill out **Item, Description, Quantity, Unit of Measure (U/M), Rate/Price, and Amount**
- Customize with a message or note to the vendor at the bottom
- Click **Save Close** or **Save &New** if you are continuously creating PO
- **Print and Send** the PO to the supplier

Entering Bills for Payment and Reimbursement

Having a better idea of entering a bill in QuickBooks is just a process of recording payables. It is easier to enter a bill by recording transactions that you will need to reimburse in the future, such as expenses, materials purchased, or any services provided by suppliers.

- *How to enter a bill:*
  - Homepage→Vendor
  - Enter bill →Select Vendor
  - Enter Invoice Date
  - Invoice Number
  - Add Description or Memo
  - Invoice Amount
  - Select Due Date(if not already setup)
  - Terms of Payment, ex. (Net 30)

Inventory Management

- *Create New Item, Adjust the Quantity, and Value in the Stock*

An inventory item is a classified product purchased for resale. It will be tracked in stock/warehouse and accounted for in the balance sheet

QuickBooks Applications
Employees supplier/list/vendors for managing payables and inventory

under current asset categories.

In order to create a new inventory item/part:

> ➤ From homepage menu go to **Vendors→Inventory Activities**
> ➤ You can create from Inventory **Center or New Item**
> ➤ Select Type as **Inventory Part.**

The below exampleis a product "Cover Sheet" to produce a notebook stored in a stock.

Whenever you see changes in the inventory as a result of damages, loss, or any other cause such as giving away as a gift or sample to customers, you need to manually adjust inventory to for an updated balance account in the stock record:

> ➤ Adjust **Quantity→Vendors** and then Inventory Activities
> ➤ Select **Adjust Quantity/Value** on Hand
> ➤ Select the **Adjustment Type**

QuickBooks Applications
Employees supplier/list/vendors for managing payables and inventory

> ➤ **▼ drop-down**, then select **Quantity, Total Value**, or **Quantity and Total Value**
>
> ➤ Select the **Adjustment Type** Option and then select **Adjustment Account.**

Check physical inventory in stock

Physical check inventory is a process that can verify quantity on hand, available, or in stock vs. quantity showing on the account or record. You can do physical count at the end of every month or any specific period to better understand your inventory status.

To do this, you can go to:

- Vendors
- Inventory Activities
- Physical Inventory Worksheet

Below is an example of a physical count that you can print and then go to the warehouse/stock and do the matching with each product. If there is any difference, write it down on "Physical Count," and once done, go ahead and make the adjustment as stated in the previous section.

Zoivu Co
Physical Inventory Worksheet
May 4, 2020

Item	Description	Preferred Vendor	Quantity On Hand	Physical Count
Flipchart			0	
Flipchart:Glue			450,000	
Flipchart:Sheet pad			950,000	
Flipchart:Sticker			1,950,000	
Notebook			0	
Notebook:Cover sheets			4,950,000	
Notebook:Printing ink			5,000	
Notebook:Stitching wire			900,000	
Notebook:Wood free paper	Wood free writing paper		950,000	
Pen			0	
Pen:Brass Tip			950,000	
Pen:Ink			950,000	
Pen:Polystyrene	Finance workshop tax		2,500	
Pen:Tube and cap			950,000	
Pen:Tungsten carbide	Tungsten carbide- a b...		950,000	
New Product			0	
New Product:Flipchart	Flowchart		48,000	
New Product:Notebook	Notebook (II)		48,000	
New Product:Pen	Pen (I)		48,000	

Inventory Assembly

QuickBooks Applications
Employees supplier/list/vendors for managing payables and inventory

This is the process of creating a product or selling a bundle from the raw material/parts (assembling vs. finished goods).

Assembly allows you to manufacture or sell your product as a package, and it also lets you automatically refill the purchase order.

The following are steps to take when creating an Inventory Assembly:

- Go to **List**→ Select **Item List**
- Click on the item drop-down arrow
- Select **New**
- Choose **Inventory Assembly** as the type
- Enter the **Inventory Items** included on the bill of materials
- Complete the **Assembly Details**
- Click **OK**

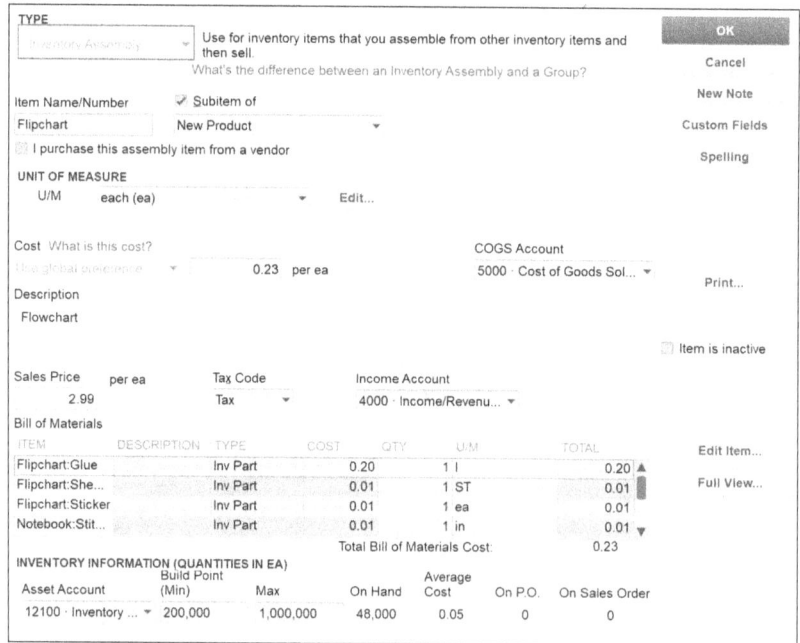

QuickBooks Applications
Employees supplier/list/vendors for managing payables and inventory

■ Managing Sales Tax

- Setup to enter expenses automatically in QuickBooks regularly
- Inventory valuation summary report

The inventory valuation summary report summarizes the quantity, average cost, and total inventory valuation.

You can get this report, as shown below, by following these steps:

➢ Go to **Reports**

➢ Inventory

➢ Inventory valuation summary

Zoivu Co
Inventory Valuation Summary
As of May 4, 2020

	On Hand	U/M	Avg Cost	Asset Value	% of Tot Asset	Sales Price	Retail Value	% of Tot Retail
Inventory								
Flipchart								
Glue	450,000	l	0.02	9,000.00	6.2%	0.00	0.00	0.0%
Sheet pad	950,000	ST	0.01	9,500.00	6.6%	0.00	0.00	0.0%
Sticker	1,950,000	ea	0.01	19,500.00	13.5%	0.00	0.00	0.0%
Flipchart - Other	0		0.00	0.00	0.0%	0.00	0.00	0.0%
Total Flipchart	3,350,000	-MIXED-		38,000.00	26.3%		0.00	0.0%
Notebook								
Cover sheets	4,950,000	ST	0.00	9,900.00	6.8%	0.00	0.00	0.0%
Printing ink	5,000	l	0.20	1,000.00	0.7%	0.00	0.00	0.0%
Stitching wire	900,000	in	0.01	9,000.00	6.2%	0.00	0.00	0.0%
Wood free paper (Wood free writing paper)	950,000	ST	0.01	9,310.00	6.4%	0.00	0.00	0.0%
Notebook - Other	0		0.00	0.00	0.0%	0.00	0.00	0.0%
Total Notebook	6,805,000	-MIXED-		29,210.00	20.2%		0.00	0.0%
Pen								
Brass Tip	950,000	ea	0.01	9,500.00	6.6%	0.00	0.00	0.0%
Ink	950,000	oz	0.01	9,500.00	6.6%	0.00	0.00	0.0%
Polystyrene	2,500	lb	5.00	12,500.00	8.6%	0.00	0.00	0.0%
Tube and cap	950,000	ea	0.01	9,500.00	6.6%	0.00	0.00	0.0%
Tungsten carbide (Tungsten carbide- a ball point)	950,000	ea	0.01	9,500.00	6.6%	0.00	0.00	0.0%
Pen - Other	0		0.00	0.00	0.0%	0.00	0.00	0.0%
Total Pen	3,802,500	-MIXED-		50,500.00	34.9%		0.00	0.0%
Total Inventory	13,957,500	-MIXED-		117,710.00	81.4%		0.00	0.0%
Assembly								
New Product								
Flipchart (Flowchart)	48,000	ea	0.05	2,400.00	1.7%	2.99	143,520.00	30.0%
Notebook (Notebook (II))	48,000	ea	0.22	10,646.40	7.4%	3.99	191,520.00	40.0%
Pen (Pen (I))	48,000	ea	0.29	13,920.00	9.6%	2.99	143,520.00	30.0%
New Product - Other	0		0.00	0.00	0.0%	0.00	0.00	0.0%
Total New Product	144,000	ea		26,966.40	18.6%		478,560.00	100.0%
Total Assembly	144,000	ea		26,966.40	18.6%		478,560.00	100.0%
TOTAL	**14,101,500**	**-MIXED-**		**144,676.40**	**100.0%**		**478,560.00**	**100.0%**

Creating And Setting Up Customers

A *customer* is a person or entity willing to purchase a product or service from the business and pays for the product or service provided.

■ Creating New Customer Account

There are also *different* other methods that you can enter or create customer in QuickBooks rather than manually enter each and every one of your customer such and those method are by copying data in batches that allows you to enter multiple list entries and even you can copy and paste the list directly from Excel file or by importing data using various files or other program.

Simple steps to add new customer:

- ➢ Go to QuickBooks homepage menu > click on **Customer**
- ➢ Click on customer center
- ➢ Click the "New Customer and Job" then select new customer from drop-down
- ➢ Enter the details such name, address and terms …etc.
- ➢ Remember the more information input the better output and once

QuickBooks Applications

Creating and setting up customers

■ Creating Estimates or Quotations

An estimate is used to create a bid, proposal, or quotation, and it can also be turned into a sales order or an invoice after the customer approves or agrees upon it.

Use the following steps to create Estimates:

- ➢ From homepage go to →**Customers**
- ➢ Select **Create Estimate**
- ➢ Select **Optional Customer** you want to create estimate for. If new customer →**Add New**
- ➢ Fill out the relevant information including **Date** and **Estimate Number**
- ➢ Enter the details (i.e. item quantity or rate proposed)
- ➢ **Discounts** (percentage or fixed amount) can also be added

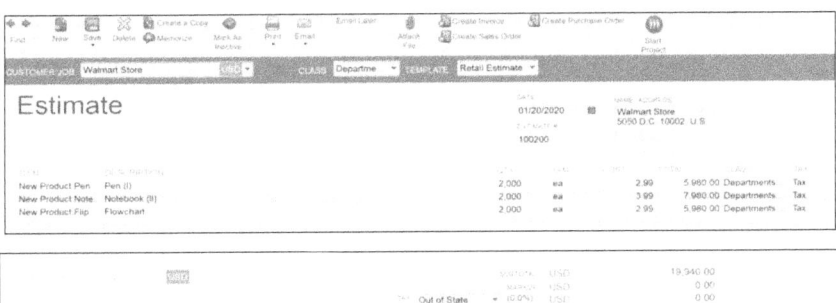

■ Creating Sales Orders

A sales order is one purchase order (PO) you send to a supplier for the purchase of goods or services. Here, we discuss the sales order (SO), which can be used to record a sale that you want to fulfill. You, as the seller, will receive this from your customer.

The difference between purchase orders and sales orders is that the purchase order will be part of your usual account payables workflow in QuickBooks desktop. In contrast, a sales order is part of your account receivables workflow depending upon which type of QuickBooks you use,

QuickBooks Applications

Creating and setting up customers

as the sales order functions in Premier and Enterprise.

To create a sales order, follow the steps below:

- Sign in as an admin and then Go to homepage →**Edit**
- **Preferences**
- Sales &Customers →**Company Preferences**
- **Enable Sales Order** and then click "**OK**"

Go back to homepage →**Customer**

- **Sales orders/Create sales orders**
- From customer: Job select a customer job (optional, or you can "Add New")
- Enter **transaction details, date, and S.O. number**
- **Save & Close**

You can also create sales orders from an estimate previously created for your client:

- Open the existing estimate by selecting **Create sales order**
- Once S.O. appears, edit it as you wish
- **Save & Close**

QuickBooks Applications

Creating and setting up customers

■ *Creating sales orders from an estimate:*

An estimate is a non-posting transaction that used to provide quotation from a supplier or to a customer that works as a proposal of project rate or price of product or services. In business estimate that also known as quotation will helps you keep track of quoted sales price.

QuickBooks Applications

Creating and setting up customers

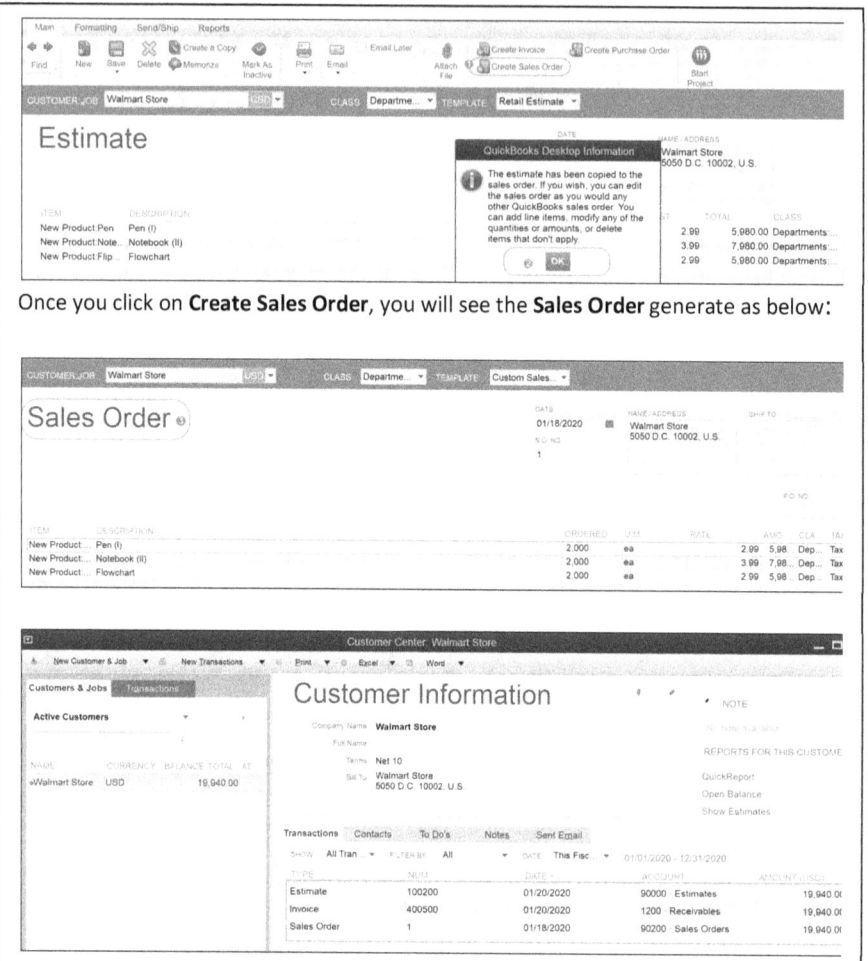

Once you click on **Create Sales Order**, you will see the **Sales Order** generate as below:

Creating Invoices and Sales Receipt (Selling on Cash/Credit)

Both **invoices** and **sales receipts** are completely different things. If your sale is in cash and you haven't received the money within the time of your sale, you can create a sales receipt that applies the cash basis of accounting. If your sale is on credit, you need to create the invoice in order to record the sales first. Then, whenever a customer pays, you can record the payments against that invoice.

To create an invoice, follow the steps below:

QuickBooks Applications
Creating and setting up customers

- Go to homepage → Customers
- Create invoice or (CRL+I)
- Complete the fields with necessary information
- Save & Close or Save &New

To create a Sales Receipt, follow the steps below:

With a Sales Receipt, enter the payment information at the same time you enter the sale

- Go to homepage → Customers
- Enter Sales Receipts
- Select the name of customer
- Enter the necessary information
- Save & Close or Save &New

Creating Statements and Assessing Finance Charges

A **statement** is a summary of your customer's account which lists invoices, credit memos, payments received, and the final balance. At the end of every month (or as necessary), you can send a statement to your customer that will show how much they owe on each invoice. However, you can also ask your suppliers to ask for a statement on how much you owe them on each invoice.

- In order to create a statement, go to the **Customers** menu:
- Choose **create statement**
- Customize it the way you wish to crate statement
- You can print it or email directly to your customer

QuickBooks Applications

Creating and setting up customers

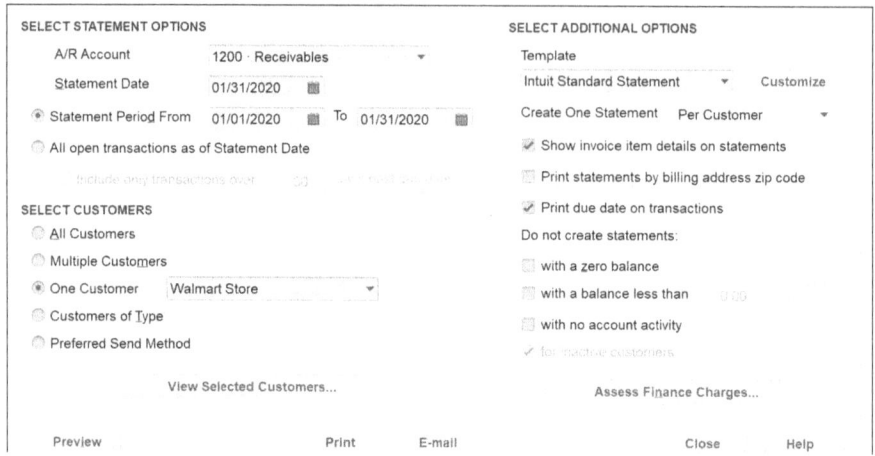

- Assessing your finance charges happens if you receive fines, late fees, or interest on unpaid balances. Prior to this, you may need to go to **Edit >Preferences>Finance Charges** to customize these in order to assess the charges.

  > Go to homepage →**Customer**

  > Choose the appropriate A/R account (note that QuickBooks displays the A/R account)

  > Set **assessment date**

  > Select the **customers jobs** you want to apply finance charges

  > Select **assess charges** and the invoice will automatically be generated on selected customer

  > You can either print or leave it blank to be included in the next statements

The statement is ready, as shown below:

QuickBooks Applications

Creating and setting up customers

Statement

Zoivu Co
ABC Drive
Nashville, TN 37211

Date: 1/31/2020

To:
Walmart Store
5050 D.C. 10002, U.S.

Amount Due	Amount Enc.
USD 19,940.00	

Date	Transaction	Amount	Balance
12/31/2019	Balance forward		0.00
01/20/2020	INV #400500, Due 01/30/2020.	19,940.00	19,940.00
	--- Pen, 2,000 @ USD 2.99 = 5,980.00		
	--- Notebook, 2,000 @ USD 3.99 = 7,980.00		
	--- Flipchart, 2,000 @ USD 2.99 = 5,980.00		
	--- Tax: Out of State @ 0.0% = 0.00		

CURRENT	1-30 DAYS PAST DUE	31-60 DAYS PAST DUE	61-90 DAYS PAST DUE	OVER 90 DAYS PAST DUE	Amount Due
0.00	19,940.00	0.00	0.00	0.00	USD 19,940.00

QuickBooks Applications

Creating and setting up customers

■ Receiving Payments via Cash, Check, Debit or E-Check Against Invoice

Receiving payment from a customer is when you make a sale by providing products or services, either in cash or credit. Use the following steps to enter payment from a customer:

- ➢ Go to QuickBooks homepage →**Customers**
- ➢ Receive **Payments**
- ➢ From the drop-down menu, select the customer's name you're receiving money from
- ➢ Enter the $ amount received
- ➢ Check the accuracy of data and method of payment such as:
    - Cash
    - Check
    - Credit/Debit
    - E-check or more
- ➢ Select the invoice (S) you would like to apply against
- ➢ Fill out other information needed, such as "tick mark left side on the date and reference no.," etc.
- ➢ **Save and close** or continue receiving payment →**Save and new**

Note: You can also enter a partial payment based on your agreement and terms with the customer.

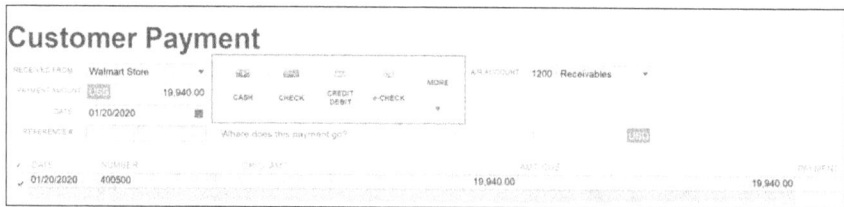

Recording Refunds and Credits Refunded to Customer

You can record a refund for goods or services that did not satisfy a customer. You can use refund receipts if a customer asks for a refund for an item or service.

How to refund processing:

- Open company file
- Homepage (icon)→**Customer**→**Create Credit Memos/Refunds**
- Enter the appropriate customer name and amount supposed to be refunded
- **Save and close**
- In the available credit window, select **Give a refund**, chose a type of card to be refunded
- Hit **OK** to process a refund.

Automatic Invoice Entry "Memories"

If you send out invoices on a regular basis by scheduling recurring invoices, QuickBooks will take care of the rest.

For instance: You have many customers that you service and would like QuickBooks to automatically email the invoices to your customers at the end of the month for $100 over the next 12 months. It also applies on a subscription basis, rental, electricity bills, or other services.

Follow these steps to create an automatic invoice entry:

- From homepage →**Customer**
- Create an invoice for the first month and then the next 11 months →**Set as Automatically**
- Open the created invoice →click on "**Memorize**" button on the top left corner
- **Name**→ Select the "**Automatic Transaction Entry**"→**Monthly**. Date it one month after (i.e. the current invoice date is (01/20/2020), the next should be (02/20/2020), number remaining → 11 more months, days to be sent 5 prior)
- Click **OK**

QuickBooks Applications

Creating and setting up customers

a

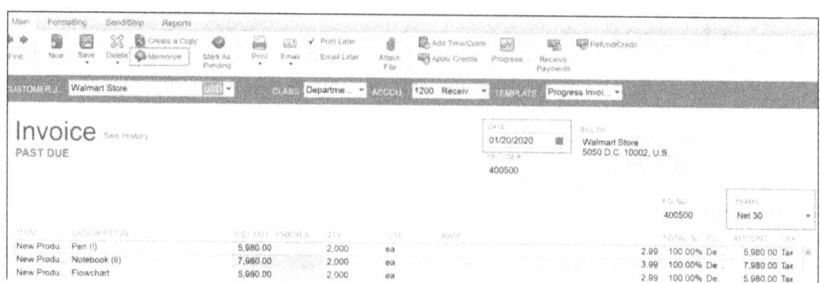

b

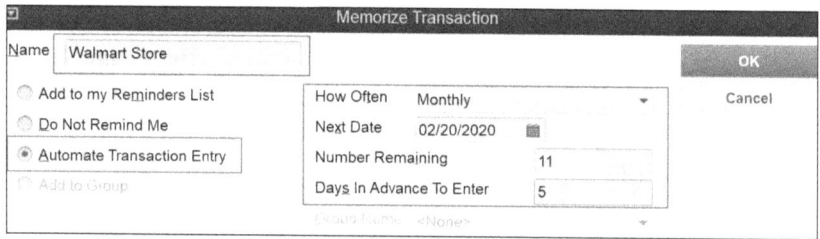

Adding Jobs and Applying Multiple Projects

Suppose you have a customer for which you perform different jobs. In order to separate those categories of tasks and clarify how much revenue is generated from each of the activities, you can create a cost report that is allocated to each of the projects.

Use the following steps to add jobs and apply multiple projects:

- ➢ From the homepage, go to **Customer Center**
- ➢ Locate customer you want to add job
- ➢ Right click on the customer and "**add a job**"
- ➢ In the job window, you can enter information about the job
- ➢ Click "**OK**" to process a complete job

For example: We have one customer listed as a "Walmart Store." We decide to sell them products and offer them an "aftersales" service (it can be named anything of your preference).

QuickBooks Applications

Creating and setting up customers

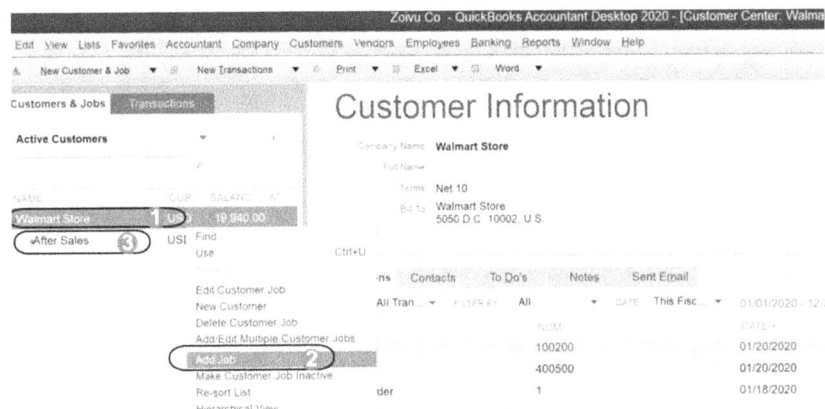

The next time you create an invoice for any aftersales service you provide to Walmart, you can simply create an invoice under "Walmart Store/After Sales." This makes it much easier to give your income statement report by job/costing for decision making.

Customizing Your Invoice and Other Forms

You can customize invoices that fit your business style, requirements, sales receipt, estimates or quotations, statements, and purchase orders.

For example: To customize an invoice for Zoivu Co.,

- ➢ Go to QuickBooks homepage →**Customers** and follow the next steps:
- ➢ **Create invoice**
- ➢ Before entering any other information, click on "**Template**." There are some built-in invoice templates listed as the following:
    - Attorney's invoice
    - Fixed fee invoice
    - Intuit packing slip
    - Intuit professional invoice
    - Intuit service invoice
    - i. Intuit standard pledge
    - ii. Invoice from proposal

QuickBooks Applications

Creating and setting up customers

    iii.   Progress invoice
    iv.   Time and expense invoice

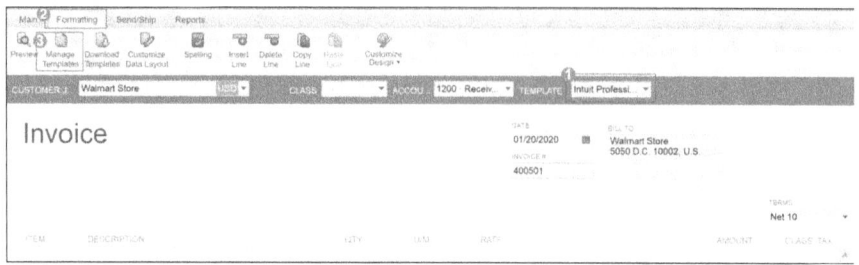

▪ Adding Logos and Customizing Invoices

With access to templates, you can further customize the invoice and add a logo and space for a signature:

> ➢ Double click on the invoice template you want to customize →**Intuit Professional Invoice**
> ➢ Select **Formatting** tab→**Manage Templates**
> ➢ Customize to your preference
> ➢ You can add a logo by clicking "**Logo**" on the invoice
> ➢ Click on phone number, email, and website address if you wish to add those fields as well
> ➢ You can use additional customization or →**Layout Designer**

QuickBooks Applications

Creating and setting up customers

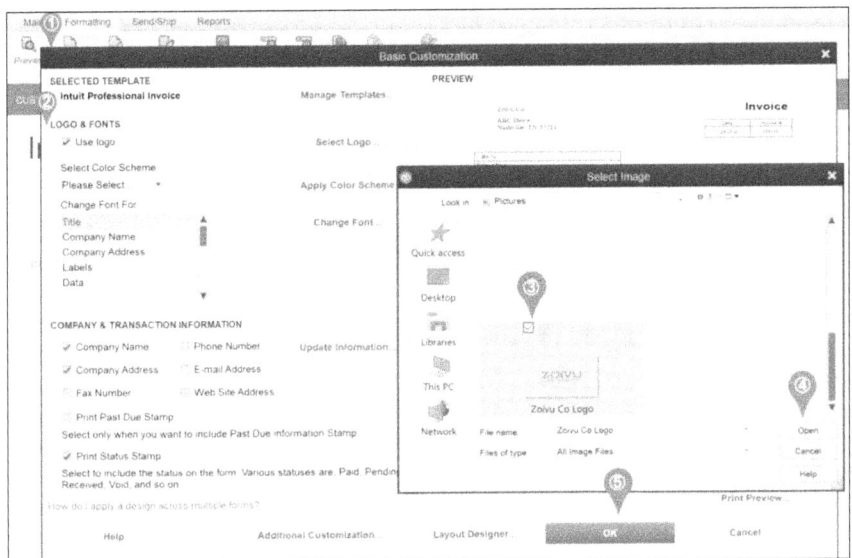

Below is how an invoice looks after customization. The following items have been added:

- Logo
- Phone number
- Email address
- Website

QuickBooks Applications

Creating and setting up customers

zoivu

Zoivu Co
ABC Drive
Nashville, TN 37211

Invoice

Date	Invoice #
1/20/2020	400501

Bill To
Walmart Store
5050 D.C. 10002, U.S.

Description	Amount
Out-of-state sale, exempt from sales tax	0.00

Total USD 0.00

Phone #	E-mail	Web Site
615.000.0000	zoivu@co.com	www.zoivu.com

Banking and Reconciliation

In order to reconcile, you need to compare a list of transactions on your bank statement vs. the information in QuickBooks. Both transactions should be balanced, and in case of a discrepancy, it needs to be corrected.

In some cases, a fee has been charged from the bank, but that amount is missing in the system, which causes a discrepancy. Thus, you need to adjust and enter that amount as a bank charge expense, which is like balancing your checkbook to match your bank and credit card statements.

- For reconciliation, go to the homepage menu →**Banking**
- Select the option "**Reconcile**"
- Select the account to be reconciled (i.e. "1010. Checking BOA")
- Find the bank statement and enter the **ending date**
- Enter **the ending balance** of your statement and ensure it matches with the correct month
- Be mindful of service charges or interest earned boxes and enter them (if any)
- Click **continue→Review** to match all
- Once done, click the "**Reconcile Now**" button to proceed

QuickBooks Applications
Banking and reconciliation

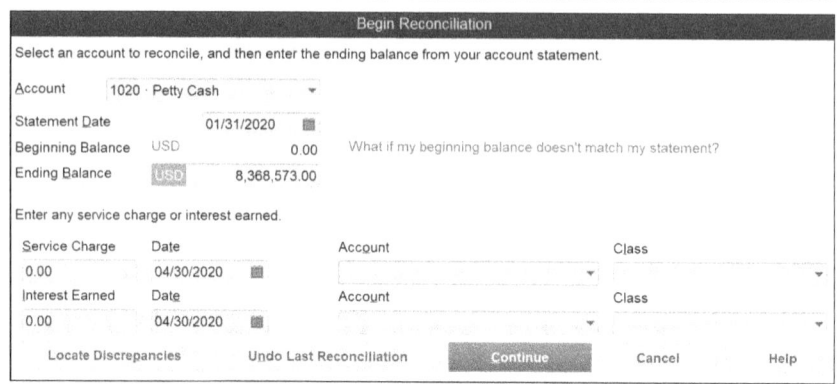

Making Journal Entries: Double Entry Bookkeeping

General Journal Entry is the method that accountants and managers use to make adjustments and double-entry accounting in books. However, it requires a fundamental accounting concept or Debit and Credit techniques in order to make a journal entry.

How it works:

- ➢ Enter Debit and Credit manually the same way as a traditional accounting system in an Excel spreadsheet or any book
- ➢ You can do adjustment entry, transfer money from one account to another, or any double entry
- ➢ Go to the homepage →**Company**:
- ➢ Make **General Journal Entries**
- ➢ Enter the necessary information in the fields (Debit & Credit should be balanced on both sides)
    - **Save & Close**

QuickBooks Applications

Banking and reconciliation

Finding & Searching Transactions and Other Information Faster (Invoice, Bill, PO)

By using "Find," you can find anything such as invoice, estimate, sales receipt, credit memo, bill, check, credit card, purchase order, or sales order.

For example: If you are looking to find a related customer by entering their first or last name, date range, invoice number, or amount, you can locate it. There is also an advance feature filter.

Let's find invoice number #400500 to learn more about this invoice:

- Go to the homepage menu →**Edit** and select **Find**
- Select transaction type as "**invoice**"
- Enter invoice number **400500**→click on the "**Find**" button
- See images below with steps for further details

QuickBooks Applications

Banking and reconciliation

Step one: Enter the information to find

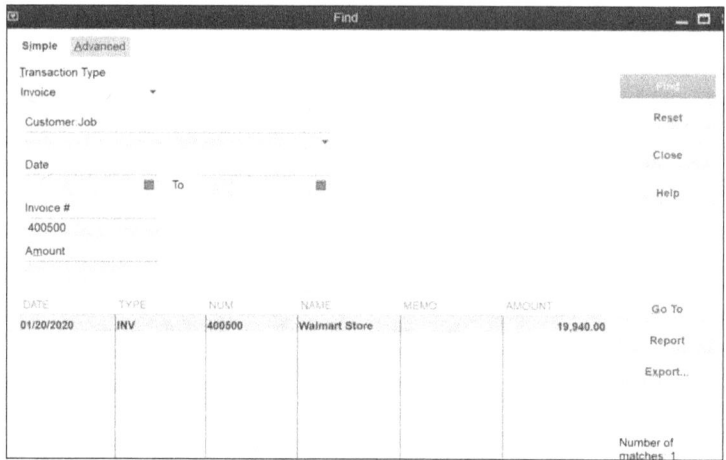

Step two: Double click on the green line to open the transaction (invoice)

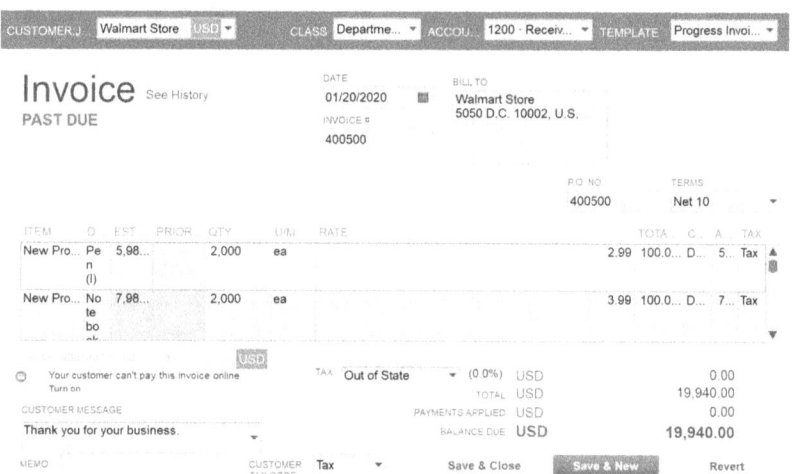

8

Reporting In QuickBooks

One of the key advantages of QuickBooks is its accuracy with reporting. Reporting is the output that provides many accounting and financial reports for household, business owners, and professional workers. All these reports can be accessed through the QuickBooks **reports** menu.

Some of the reports you can obtain from QuickBooks are as follows:

- Company and Financial: Including profit and loss standard, profit and loss details, balance sheet standard, and detail.

QuickBooks Applications
Reporting in QuickBooks

- *Customers and Receivable:* Including Account Receivable (AR) aging summary, AR detail, and open invoice.
- *Sales Reports:* Including sales by customer summary, sales by customer details
- *Jobs, Time and Millage:* Including job profitability summary, job probability detail, and estimates by job.
- *Vendors and Payables:* Account Payables (AP) aging summary, AP aging detail, vendor balance summary, vendor balance detail, and unpaid bills detail.
- *Purchase Reports:* You can get report of purchase by vendor summary, purchase by vendor detail and open purchase orders that haven't been fulfilled yet.
- *Inventory Reports:* Including inventory valuation summary, and inventory valuation detail report.
- *Employees and Payroll:* Including payroll summary, payroll item details, and workers comp summary.
- *Banking Reports:* Deposit detail report, check detail, missing checks, reconciliation discrepancy and previous reconciliation.
- *Accountant and Taxes:* Including Trial Balance (TB), general ledger, and audit trial report.
- *List:* Including an account listing report, price listing, customer phone list, vendor phone list, and terms list.
- *Manufacturing and Wholesale Edition Reports:* Sales by rep detail, sales by product, and open sales order by customer.
- *Non-Profit Edition Reports:* These include the biggest donors or grants, budget vs. actual by donors/grants.
- *Professional Services Edition Reports:* Billed or unbilled hours by person, project costs details and project status.
- *Retail Edition Reports:* These are profit and loss monthly comparisons, sales graphs, and accounts payable graphs.

Company and Financial: These reports are profit and loss standard, profit and loss details, balance sheet standard, and detail.

QuickBooks Applications

Reporting in QuickBooks

Profit and loss shows your company or personal income, direct cost, expense, and net income or loss over a specific time. Below is a guide on how to get a report of standard income and detail from QuickBooks:

- From the homepage menu go to Reports
- Company and Financial → Profit and Loss

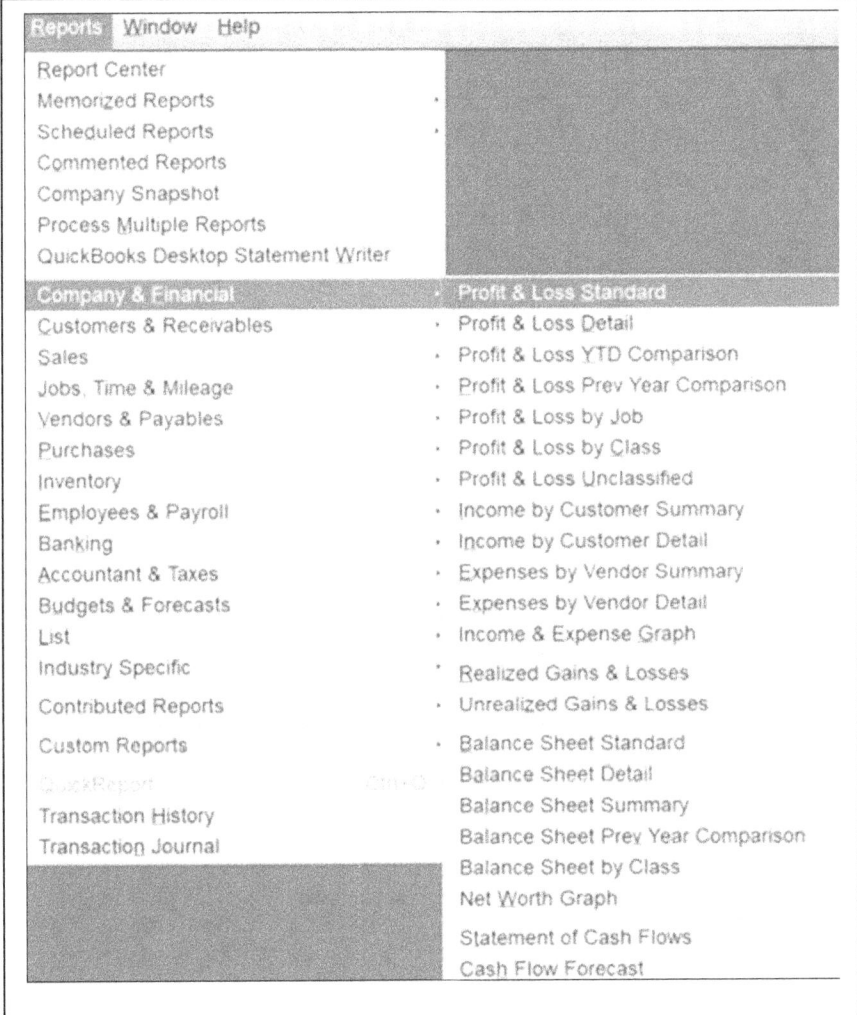

Profit and Loss Standard:

When you look at the Zoivu Co. P&L Standard for the month of Jan. 2020, you can see that the total income is $19,990, the total cost of goods sold (COGS) is $18,866.40, and the net income (loss) is listed as -

QuickBooks Applications

Reporting in QuickBooks

$61,203.60, which indicates a loss.

The date highlighted below shows that you can also select custom date for any month or year of your company or personal financial report:

Dates Custom   From 01/01/2020   To 01/31/2020

Report Basis: ● Accrual ○ Cash   Show Filters

11:43 PM
05/23/20
Accrual Basis

Zoivu Co
Profit & Loss
January 2020

	Jan 20
Income	
4000 · Income/Revenue	
4010 · Sales of Pen	5,980.00
4020 · Sales of Notebook	7,980.00
4030 · Sales Flipchart	5,980.00
Total 4000 · Income/Revenue	19,940.00
Total Income	19,940.00
Cost of Goods Sold	
5000 · Cost of Goods Sold (COGS)	
5010 · COGS of Pen	580.00
5020 · COGS of Notebook	443.60
5030 · COGS of Flipchart	100.00
Total 5000 · Cost of Goods Sold (CO...	1,123.60
Total COGS	1,123.60
Gross Profit	18,816.40
Expense	
6000 · Operational Expenses	
6010 · Advertising Expense	10,000.00
6350 · Depreciation Expense	6,893.00
6750 · Professional Fees	200.00
7000 · Payroll Taxes	14,253.00
7250 · Repairs Expense	2,000.00
7300 · Salaries Expense	31,752.00
7500 · Utilities Expense	1,800.00
Total 6000 · Operational Expenses	66,898.00
8000 · TN Tax 9%	13,122.00
Total Expense	80,020.00
Net Income	-61,203.60

Profit and Loss Detail:

While a standard report provides only a summary and concise report, a details report provides the same but with more detailed options.

Below is an example of profit and loss details for Zoivu Co., with the same end of -$61,000, indicating loss for the month of January.

QuickBooks Applications

Reporting in QuickBooks

Balance Sheet Standard Report

A balance sheet is also named as a financial position, which is a snapshot of your company or personal financial position at a specific time by showing your asset value, liabilities, and capital. In a balance sheet, your total asset values should always equal your liability deduction owner's equality.

```
11:49 PM                                    Zoivu Co
05/23/20                              Profit & Loss Detail
Accrual Basis                           All Transactions

   Type          Date     Num  Adj    Name          Memo        Class   Clr    Split        Debit      Credit     Balance
   Invoice     01/20/2020 400       Walmart Store   Flowchart   Depart        1200 Rece                5,950.00   5,980.00
   Total 4030 · Sales Flipchart                                                                0.00    5,980.00   5,980.00
   4800 · Finance Charge Income
   Invoice     05/20/2020 FC 1      Walmart Store   Finance Ch                1200 Rece                   50.00      50.00
   Total 4800 · Finance Charge Income                                                          0.00       50.00      50.00
   Total 4000 · Income/Revenue                                                                 0.00   19,990.00  19,990.00
   Total Income                                                                                0.00   19,990.00  19,990.00
   Cost of Goods Sold
     5000 · Cost of Goods Sold (COGS)
       5010 · COGS of Pen
   Invoice     01/20/2020 400       Walmart Store   Pen (I)     Depart        1200 Rece      580.00                  580.00
   Total 5010 · COGS of Pen                                                                  580.00        0.00     580.00
       5020 · COGS of Notebook
   Invoice     01/20/2020 400       Walmart Store   Notebook (  Depart        1200 Rece      443.60                  443.60
   Total 5020 · COGS of Notebook                                                             443.60        0.00     443.60
       5030 · COGS of Flipchart
   Invoice     01/20/2020 400       Walmart Store   Flowchart   Depart        1200 Rece      100.00                  100.00
   Total 5030 · COGS of Flipchart                                                            100.00        0.00     100.00
     Total 5000 · Cost of Goods Sold (COGS)                                                1,123.60        0.00   1,123.60
   Total COGS                                                                              1,123.60        0.00   1,123.60
   Gross Profit                                                                            1,123.60   19,990.00  18,866.40
   Expense
     6000 · Operational Expenses
       6010 · Advertising Expense
   Bill        01/18/2020           CNBC TV         TV advertis               2100 Paya   10,000.00               10,000.00
   Total 6010 · Advertising Expense                                                       10,000.00        0.00  10,000.00
       6350 · Depreciation Expense
   General Journal 01/31/2020 3                     Depreciatio               6350 Depr    6,893.00                6,893.00
   Total 6350 · Depreciation Expense                                                       6,893.00        0.00   6,893.00
       6750 · Professional Fees
   Bill        01/03/2020 10033     Department of Bu Business l               2100 Paya      200.00                  200.00
   Total 6750 · Professional Fees                                                            200.00        0.00     200.00
       7000 · Payroll Taxes
   General Journal 01/30/2020 2     -MULTIPLE-      Salary exp  -MULTI        7300 Sala   14,253.00               14,253.00
   Total 7000 · Payroll Taxes                                                             14,253.00        0.00  14,253.00
       7250 · Repairs Expense
   Check       01/15/2020 111       D D Decor       New office               1010 Chec    2,000.00                2,000.00
   Total 7250 · Repairs Expense                                                            2,000.00        0.00   2,000.00
       7300 · Salaries Expense
   General Journal 01/30/2020 2     -MULTIPLE-      Salary exp  -MULTI        7300 Sala   31,752.00               31,752.00
   Total 7300 · Salaries Expense                                                          31,752.00        0.00  31,752.00
       7500 · Utilities Expense
   Bill        01/25/2020 008       Nashville Electric Electricity b          2100 Paya    1,800.00                1,800.00
   Total 7500 · Utilities Expense                                                          1,800.00        0.00   1,800.00
     Total 6000 · Operational Expenses                                                    66,898.00        0.00  66,898.00
     8000 · TN Tax 9%
   Bill        01/12/2020 556       BP Group        TN Tax 9%   Depart        2100 Paya   13,122.00               13,122.00
   Total 8000 · TN Tax 9%                                                                 13,122.00        0.00  13,122.00
   Total Expense                                                                          80,020.00        0.00  80,020.00
   Net Income                                                                             81,143.60   19,990.00 -61,153.60
```

To find the owner's equity or capital, deduct total assets from your total liability, which shows the net worth of your asset. You can follow the same steps you did for getting P&L from QuickBooks. The circled total below assets $9,539,996.40 equal to liability and equity.

QuickBooks Applications

Reporting in QuickBooks

12:00 AM
05/24/20
Accrual Basis

Zoivu Co
Balance Sheet
As of January 31, 2020

	Jan 31, 20
1300 · Inventories	
1310 · Work-in-Progress	13,920.00
1320 · Finished Goods	10,646.40
Total 1300 · Inventories	24,566.40
1400 · Preapid Expense	
1410 · Prepaid Insurance	1,200.00
1420 · Prepaid Rental	10,500.00
Total 1400 · Preapid Expense	11,700.00
1430 · Deposit	70,000.00
Total Other Current Assets	226,376.40
Total Current Assets	**8,792,689.40**
Fixed Assets	
1500 · Property Plant & Equipment (PPE	
1510 · PPE - Building	200,000.00
1520 · PPE- Machinary & Equipment	150,000.00
1530 · PPE- Vehicles	90,000.00
1540 · PPE- Computer and Equipment	12,000.00
1550 · PPE - Furniture & Fixture	22,200.00
1560 · PPE - Leasehold Improvement	280,000.00
1600 · Accumulated Depreciation & Amor	-2,076.00
1610 · Accum Depre Building	-2,771.00
1630 · Accum Depre Vehicle	-1,492.00
1640 · Accum Depre Computer Equipment	-554.00
Total 1500 · Property Plant & Equipment (P...	747,307.00
Total Fixed Assets	747,307.00
TOTAL ASSETS	**9,539,996.40**
LIABILITIES & EQUITY	
Liabilities	
Current Liabilities	
Accounts Payable	
2100 · Payables	601,200.00
Total Accounts Payable	601,200.00
Total Current Liabilities	601,200.00
Total Liabilities	601,200.00
Equity	
3000 · Owners Equities	
3100 · Investment from George	3,000,000.00
3200 · Investment from Michael	3,000,000.00
3300 · Investment Charlies	3,000,000.00
Total 3000 · Owners Equities	9,000,000.00
Net Income	-61,203.60
Total Equity	8,938,796.40
TOTAL LIABILITIES & EQUITY	**9,539,996.40**

Customers and Receivables: Such as Account Receivable (AR) aging summary, AR detail, and open invoice.

Account Receivables shows the report when your client purchases your company's goods or services but does not pay at the time of purchase. Thus, it is the report that customers owe you.

Below are steps you can take to obtain a Receivable Account Report.

QuickBooks Applications

Reporting in QuickBooks

In AR report, you have only one customer that owes you money.

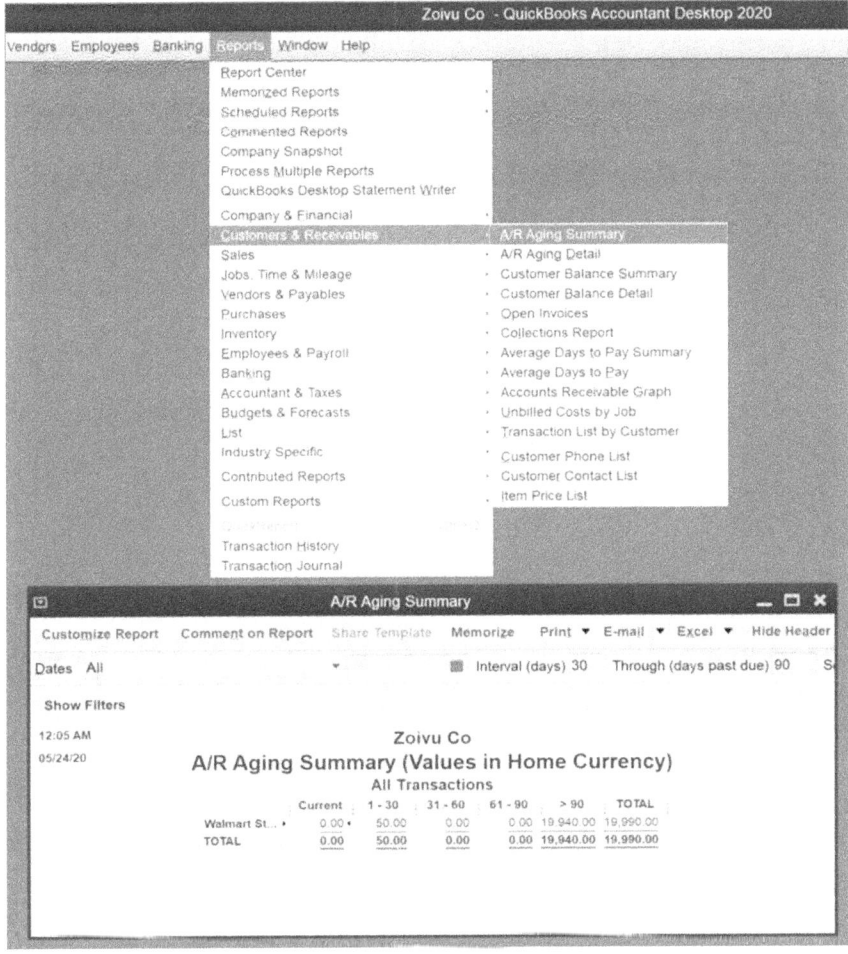

Note: The numbers listed in AR stand for account receivable as 1-30, 31-60, 61-90, >90. These are called aging, which are tools used by collections to determine which invoice is overdue for payment and how long it has been overdue (in days). However, collectors focus more on old aging, which is under the category **>90 days**.

Sales Reports: Report sales by customer summary and sales by customer details

The sales report below gives you a clear image on your billing and sales process for each customer and the products or services sold to them.

QuickBooks Applications

Reporting in QuickBooks

Vendors and Payables: Account Payables (AP) aging summary, AP aging detail, vendor balance summary, vendor balance detail, and unpaid bills detail. These reports will give you information on how much your company (or you personally) owe to your vendors or suppliers who provided goods or services on credit or later payment, similar to accounts receivable.

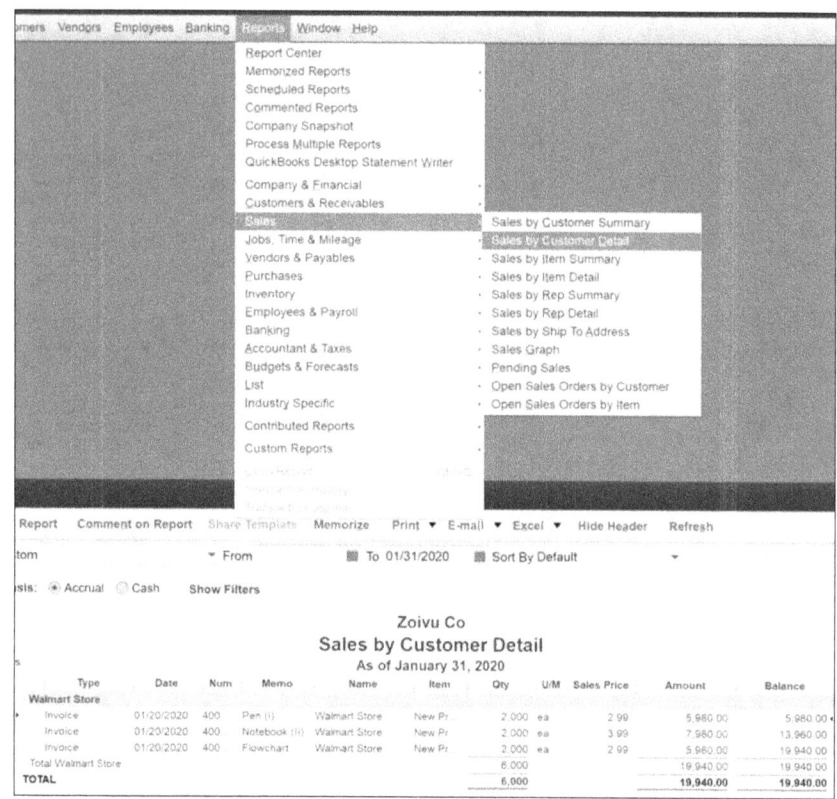

QuickBooks Applications

Reporting in QuickBooks

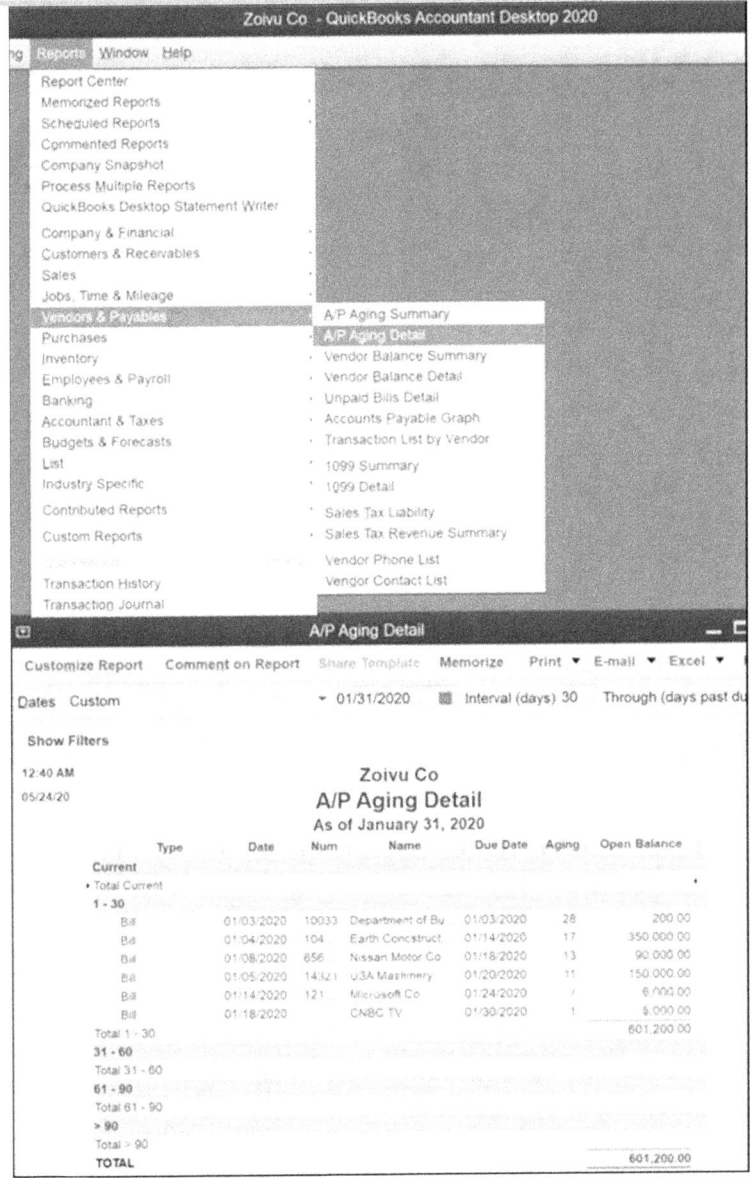

Purchase Reports: You can get a report of purchase by vendor summary, purchase by vendor detail, and open purchase orders that haven't been fulfilled yet.

This report provides you with information on the purchases you made from different suppliers, including open purchase orders. You can use customers and get different reports to show detailed information about your purchases and each item.

QuickBooks Applications

Reporting in QuickBooks

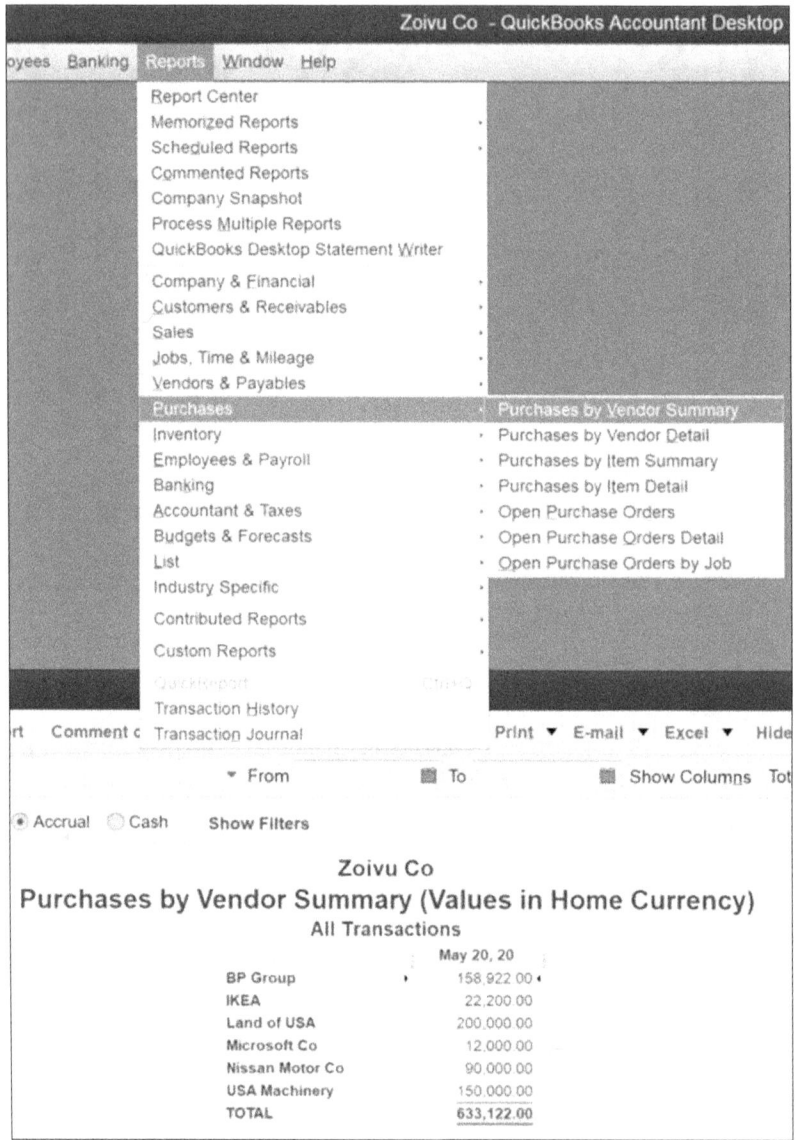

Inventory Reports: Including inventory valuation summary and an inventory valuation detail report

An inventory valuation report in QuickBooks shows the cost of your item that makes your inventory, summarized quantity, average cost on items, and extended value. That total inventory summary value is also shown in your balance sheet report under current assets and inventory.

QuickBooks Applications

Reporting in QuickBooks

Zoivu Co
Inventory Valuation Summary
As of January 31, 2020

	On Hand	U/M	Avg Cost	Asset Value	% of Tot Asset	Sales Price	Retail Value	% of Tot Retail
Inventory								
Flipchart								
Glue	450.000	i	0.02	9,000.00	6.2%	0.00	0.00	0.0%
Sheet pad	950.000	ST	0.01	9,500.00	6.6%	0.00	0.00	0.0%
Sticker	1,950.000	ea	0.01	19,500.00	13.5%	0.00	0.00	0.0%
Flipchart - Other	0		0.00	0.00	0.0%	0.00	0.00	0.0%
Total Flipchart	3,350.000	-M		38,000.00	26.3%		0.00	0.0%
Notebook								
Cover sheets	4,950.000	ST	0.00	9,900.00	6.8%	0.00	0.00	0.0%
Printing ink	5.000	i	0.20	1,000.00	0.7%	0.00	0.00	0.0%
Stitching wire	900.000	m	0.01	9,000.00	6.2%	0.00	0.00	0.0%
Wood free paper (Wood...	950.000	ST	0.01	9,310.00	6.4%	0.00	0.00	0.0%
Notebook - Other	0		0.00	0.00	0.0%	0.00	0.00	0.0%
Total Notebook	6,805.000	-M		29,210.00	20.2%		0.00	0.0%
Pen								
Brass Tip	950.000	ea	0.01	9,500.00	6.6%	0.00	0.00	0.0%
Ink	950.000	oz	0.01	9,500.00	6.6%	0.00	0.00	0.0%
Polystyrene	2.500	lb	5.00	12,500.00	8.6%	0.00	0.00	0.0%
Tube and cap	950.000	ea	0.01	9,500.00	6.6%	0.00	0.00	0.0%
Tungsten carbide (Tung...	950.000	ea	0.01	9,500.00	6.6%	0.00	0.00	0.0%
Pen - Other	0		0.00	0.00	0.0%	0.00	0.00	0.0%
Total Pen	3,802.500	-M		50,500.00	34.9%		0.00	0.0%
Total Inventory	13,957.500	-M		117,710.00	81.4%		0.00	0.0%
Assembly								
New Product								
Flipchart (Flowchart)	48.000	ea	0.05	2,400.00	1.7%	2.99	143,520.00	30.0%
Notebook (Notebook (II))	48.000	ea	0.22	10,646.40	7.4%	3.99	191,520.00	40.0%
Pen (Pen (I))	48.000	ea	0.29	13,920.00	9.6%	2.99	143,520.00	30.0%
New Product - Other	0		0.00	0.00	0.0%	0.00	0.00	0.0%
Total New Product	144.000	ea		26,966.40	18.6%		478,560.00	100.0%
Total Assembly	144.000	ea		26,966.40	18.6%		478,560.00	100.0%
TOTAL	**14,101.500**	**-M...**		**144,676.40**	**100.0%**		**478,560.00**	**100.0%**

This report is very useful when you decide whether to make purchases or whether you have enough inventory in stock.

Employees and Payroll: These reports are payroll summaries, payroll item details, and workers comp summaries.

Banking Reports: You can find information about your personal finance or business banking transactions such as Deposit detail report, check detail, missing checks, reconciliation discrepancy, and previous reconciliation.

Deposit Detail(see below)

1:05 AM
05/24/20

Zoivu Co
Deposit Detail
All Transactions

Type	Num	Date	Name	Account	Amount
General Journal	1	01/02/2020	George A	1010 · Checking...	3,000,000.00
			Michael B	1010 · Checking...	3,000,000.00
			Charles C	1010 · Checking...	3,000,000.00
			George A	3100 · Investmen...	-3,000,000.00
			Michael B	3200 · Investmen...	-3,000,000.00
			Charles C	3300 · Investmen...	-3,000,000.00
TOTAL					-3,000,000.00

QuickBooks Applications

Reporting in QuickBooks

Check Detail

Zoivu Co
Check Detail
As of January 31, 2020

1:07 AM
05/24/20

Type	Date	Name	Item	Account	Paid Amount	Original Amount
Check	01/02/2020	City Lease		1010 · Checking...		-10,500.00
				1420 Prepaid R...	-10,500.00	10,500.00
TOTAL					-10,500.00	10,500.00
Check	01/04/2020	IKEA		1020 · Petty Cash		-22,200.00
			PPE:O...	1550 PPE - Fur...	-2,500.00	2,500.00
			PPE:O...	1550 PPE - Fur...	-4,250.00	4,250.00
			PPE:Fo...	1550 PPE - Fur...	-450.00	450.00
			PPE:Rug	1550 PPE - Fur...	-15,000.00	15,000.00
TOTAL					-22,200.00	22,200.00

Accountant and Taxes: Such as Trial Balance (TB), general ledger, and audit trial report.

This report will provide you information about finances and taxes, such as adjusting journal entries, trial balances, listings of fixed assets, names listed as property plant and equipment, or (PPE) and income tax detail.

Below is an example report on Trial Balance (TB) of Zoivu Co. as of Jan 31, 2020:

QuickBooks Applications

Reporting in QuickBooks

```
Zoivu Co - QuickBooks Accountant Desktop 2020
Reports  Window  Help
  Report Center
  Memorized Reports          ▸
  Scheduled Reports          ▸
  Commented Reports          ▸
  Company Snapshot
  Process Multiple Reports
  QuickBooks Desktop Statement Writer
  Company & Financial        ▸
  Customers & Receivables    ▸
  Sales                      ▸
  Jobs, Time & Mileage       ▸
  Vendors & Payables         ▸
  Purchases                  ▸
  Inventory                  ▸
  Employees & Payroll        ▸
  Banking                    ▸
  Accountant & Taxes         ▸    • Adjusted Trial Balance
  Budgets & Forecasts        ▸    • Trial Balance
  List                       ▸    • General Ledger
  Industry Specific          ▸    • Transaction Detail by Account
  Contributed Reports        ▸    • Adjusting Journal Entries
  Custom Reports             ▸      Journal
  QuickReport        Ctrl+Q        Audit Trail
  Transaction History              Closing Date Exception Report
  Transaction Journal              Customer Credit Card Audit Trail
                                   Voided/Deleted Transactions Summary
                                   Voided/Deleted Transactions Detail
                                   Transaction List by Date
                                   Account Listing
                                   Fixed Asset Listing
                                   Income Tax Preparation
                                   Income Tax Summary
                                   Income Tax Detail
```

QuickBooks Applications

Reporting in QuickBooks

There is a difference between unadjusted trial balance and adjusted trial balance. A trial balance contains a list of general ledger accounts of the business that shows total amount on the Debit equal to Credit, which is proof that all transactions are appropriately recorded in the books.

This is shown below:

1:20 AM
05/24/20
Accrual Basis

Zoivu Co
Trial Balance
As of January 31, 2020

	Jan 31, 20	
	Debit	Credit
1010 · Checking BOA	8,368,573.00	
1020 · Petty Cash	177,800.00	
1200 · Receivables	19,940.00	
12100 · Inventory Asset	120,110.00	
1300 · Inventories:1310 · Work-in-Progress	13,920.00	
1300 · Inventories:1320 · Finished Goods	10,646.40	
1400 · Prepaid Expense:1410 · Prepaid Insurance	1,200.00	
1400 · Prepaid Expense:1420 · Prepaid Rental	10,500.00	
1430 · Deposit	70,000.00	
1500 · Property Plant & Equipment (PPE:1510 · PPE - Building	200,000.00	
1500 · Property Plant & Equipment (PPE:1520 · PPE- Machinary & Equipment	150,000.00	
1500 · Property Plant & Equipment (PPE:1530 · PPE- Vehicles	90,000.00	
1500 · Property Plant & Equipment (PPE:1540 · PPE- Computer and Equipment	12,000.00	
1500 · Property Plant & Equipment (PPE:1550 · PPE - Furniture & Fixture	22,200.00	
1500 · Property Plant & Equipment (PPE:1560 · PPE - Leasehold Improvement	280,000.00	
1500 · Property Plant & Equipment (PPE:1600 · Accumulated Depreciation & Amor		2,076.00
1500 · Property Plant & Equipment (PPE:1610 · Accum Depre Building		2,771.00
1500 · Property Plant & Equipment (PPE:1630 · Accum Depre Vehicle		1,492.00
1500 · Property Plant & Equipment (PPE:1640 · Accum Depre Computer Equipment		554.00
2100 · Payables		601,200.00
25500 · Sales Tax Payable	0.00	
3000 · Owners Equities:3100 · Investment from George		3,000,000.00
3000 · Owners Equities:3200 · Investment from Michael		3,000,000.00
3000 · Owners Equities:3300 · Investment Charlies		3,000,000.00
4000 · Income/Revenue:4010 · Sales of Pen		5,980.00
4000 · Income/Revenue:4020 · Sales of Notebook		7,980.00
4000 · Income/Revenue:4030 · Sales Flipchart		5,980.00
5000 · Cost of Goods Sold (COGS):5010 · COGS of Pen	580.00	
5000 · Cost of Goods Sold (COGS):5020 · COGS of Notebook	443.60	
5000 · Cost of Goods Sold (COGS):5030 · COGS of Flipchart	100.00	
6000 · Operational Expenses:6010 · Advertising Expense	10,000.00	
6000 · Operational Expenses:6350 · Depreciation Expense	6,893.00	
6000 · Operational Expenses:6750 · Professional Fees	200.00	
6000 · Operational Expenses:7000 · Payroll Taxes	14,253.00	
6000 · Operational Expenses:7250 · Repairs Expense	2,000.00	
6000 · Operational Expenses:7300 · Salaries Expense	31,752.00	
6000 · Operational Expenses:7500 · Utilities Expense	1,800.00	
8000 · TN Tax 9%	13,122.00	
TOTAL	**9,628,033.00**	**9,628,033.00**

List: Under lists, you can get an account listing report, price listing, customer phone list, vendor phone list, and terms list. Specifically, this report provides information about various lists in QuickBooks (such as chart of account, vendor/customer list with their contact details, list of products or services, etc.).

QuickBooks Applications

Reporting in QuickBooks

For example: If you want to download, print, email, or export in Excel, make a chart of accounts of your company:

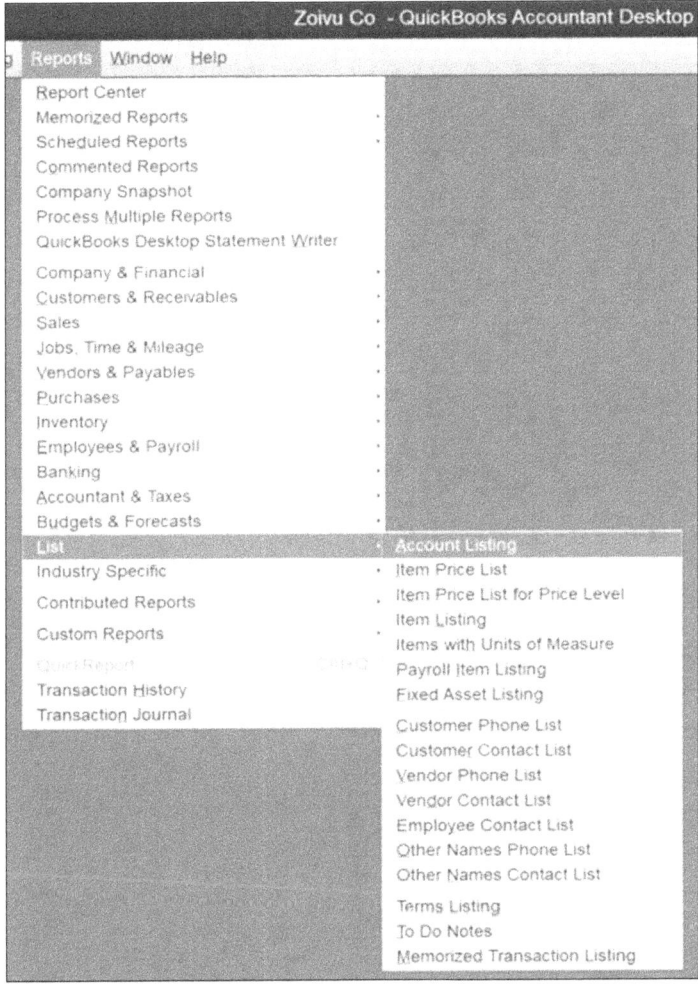

There are many ways you can customize and get information from QuickBooks. The COAchart of account below highlights how you can memorize, print, email, or export to Excel based on your need and desire.

Here is an example of a Chart of Accounts (COA):

QuickBooks Applications

Reporting in QuickBooks

```
Comment on Report   Share Template   Memorize   Print ▼   E-mail ▼   Excel ▼   Hide Header   Refresh
```

Zoivu Co
Account Listing
May 24, 2020

Account	Type	Currency
1010 · Checking BOA	Bank	USD
1020 · Petty Cash	Bank	USD
1200 · Receivables	Accounts Receivable	USD
1200 · Receivables:1210 · A/R Trade	Accounts Receivable	USD
1200 · Receivables:1220 · A/R Trade Notes Receivable	Accounts Receivable	USD
12000 · Undeposited Funds	Other Current Asset	USD
12100 · Inventory Asset	Other Current Asset	USD
1300 · Inventories	Other Current Asset	USD
1300 · Inventories:1310 · Work-in-Progress	Other Current Asset	USD
1300 · Inventories:1320 · Finished Goods	Other Current Asset	USD
1400 · Preapid Expense	Other Current Asset	USD
1400 · Preapid Expense:1410 · Prepaid Insurance	Other Current Asset	USD
1400 · Preapid Expense:1420 · Prepaid Rental	Other Current Asset	USD
1430 · Deposit	Other Current Asset	USD
1500 · Property Plant & Equipment (PPE	Fixed Asset	USD
1500 · Property Plant & Equipment (PPE:1510 · PPE - Building	Fixed Asset	USD
1500 · Property Plant & Equipment (PPE:1520 · PPE- Machinary & Equipment	Fixed Asset	USD
1500 · Property Plant & Equipment (PPE:1530 · PPE- Vehicles	Fixed Asset	USD
1500 · Property Plant & Equipment (PPE:1540 · PPE- Computer and Equipment	Fixed Asset	USD
1500 · Property Plant & Equipment (PPE:1550 · PPE - Furniture & Fixture	Fixed Asset	USD
1500 · Property Plant & Equipment (PPE:1560 · PPE - Leasehold Improvement	Fixed Asset	USD
1500 · Property Plant & Equipment (PPE:1600 · Accumulated Depreciation & Amor	Fixed Asset	USD
1500 · Property Plant & Equipment (PPE:1610 · Accum Depre Building	Fixed Asset	USD
1500 · Property Plant & Equipment (PPE:1620 · Accum Depre Machinary & Equipme	Fixed Asset	USD
1500 · Property Plant & Equipment (PPE:1630 · Accum Depre Vehicle	Fixed Asset	USD
1500 · Property Plant & Equipment (PPE:1640 · Accum Depre Computer Equipment	Fixed Asset	USD
1500 · Property Plant & Equipment (PPE:1650 · Accum Depre Furniture & Fixtures	Fixed Asset	USD
1500 · Property Plant & Equipment (PPE:1660 · Accum Depre Leasehold Improveme	Fixed Asset	USD
2100 · Payables	Accounts Payable	USD
2100 · Payables:2110 · A/P Accrued Accounts Payable	Accounts Payable	USD
2100 · Payables:2120 · Accrued - Payroll	Accounts Payable	USD
2100 · Payables:2130 · Accrued - Commissions	Accounts Payable	USD
2100 · Payables:2140 · Withholding Tax Payable	Accounts Payable	USD
2100 · Payables:2150 · AP Trade	Accounts Payable	USD
24000 · Payroll Liabilities	Other Current Liability	USD
25500 · Sales Tax Payable	Other Current Liability	USD
2700 · Long Term Debt	Long Term Liability	USD
2700 · Long Term Debt:2710 · Notes Payable	Long Term Liability	USD
2700 · Long Term Debt:2720 · Mortgages Payable	Long Term Liability	USD
2700 · Long Term Debt:2730 · Installment Notes Payable	Long Term Liability	USD
3000 · Owners Equities	Equity	USD
3000 · Owners Equities:3100 · Investment from George	Equity	USD
3000 · Owners Equities:3200 · Investment from Michael	Equity	USD

Company Snapshot

This panel provides real-time and consolidated information about your company performance task from a single place with different graphs and charts. You can see three snapshot tabs available, which are all company snapshots that show all consolidated, payment, and customer snapshots. However, you can always customize them based on your preferences.

QuickBooks Applications

Reporting in QuickBooks

Category (1):

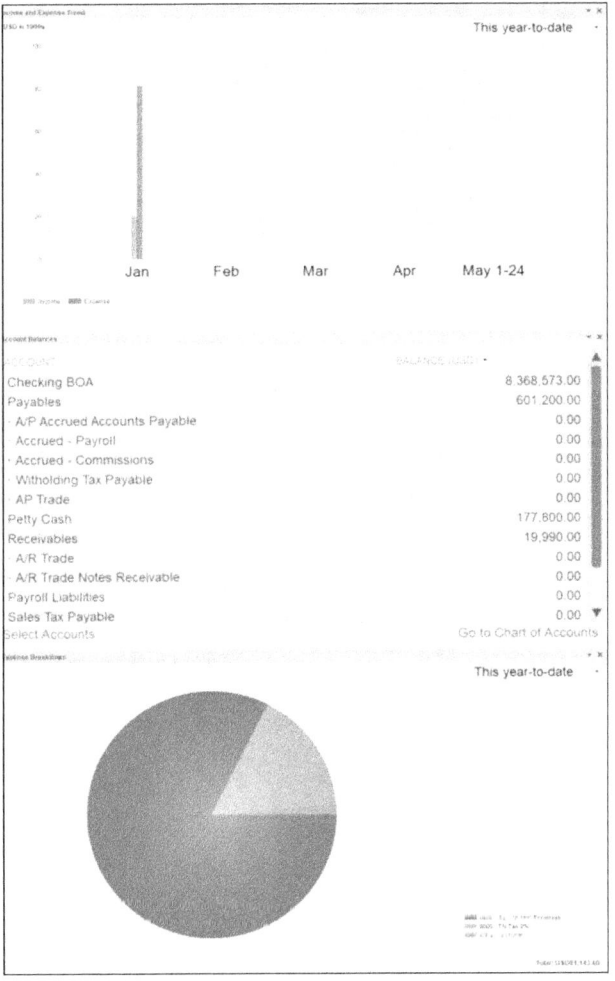

QuickBooks Applications

Reporting in QuickBooks

Category (II):

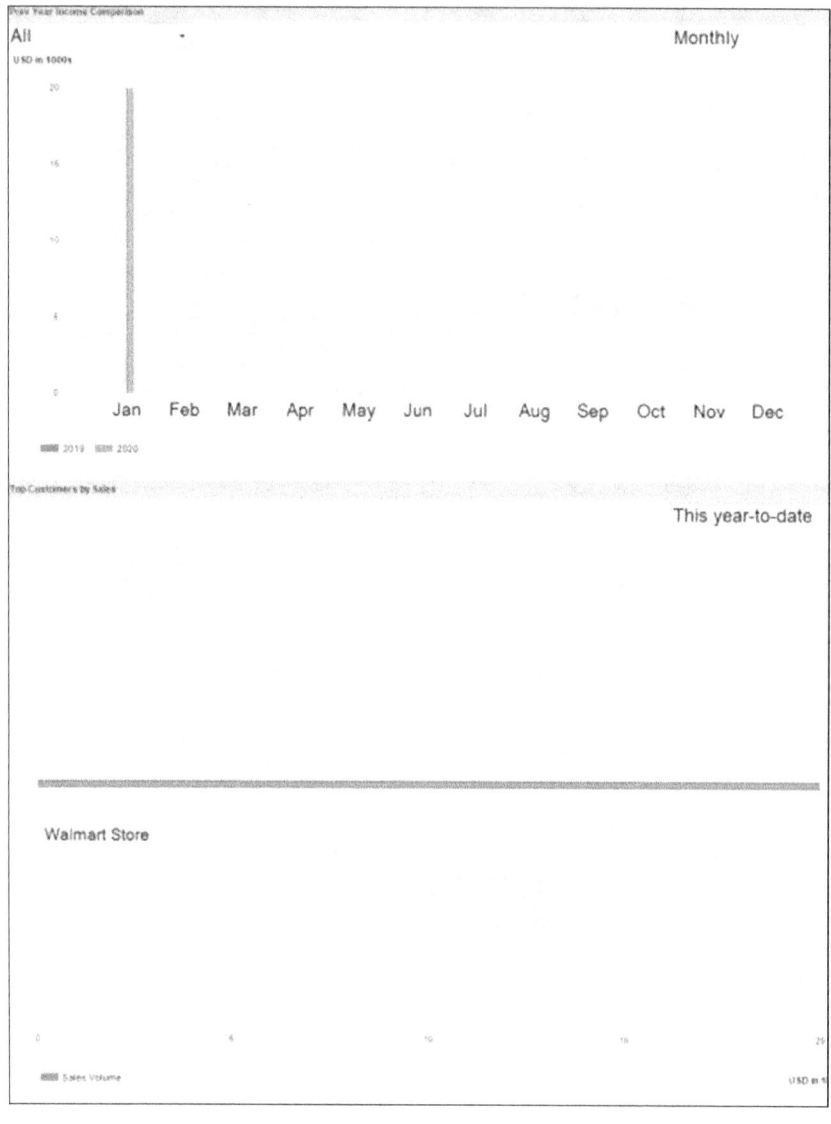

Category (III):

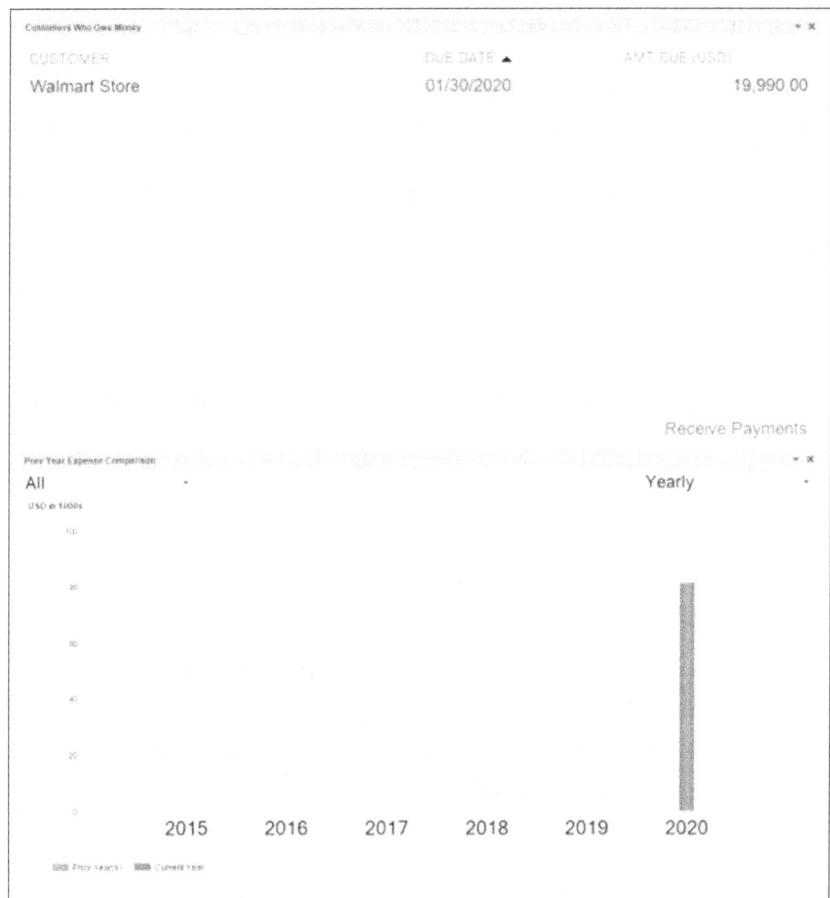

Budgeting and Forecasting

Before you enter a budget in QuickBooks, let's begin understanding the budget itself. Budget is a future activities financial plan in your business by predicting your revenues, expenses, and cash. In QuickBooks, you can use a budgeting and forecasting tool to enable you to plan and make better and smarter business decisions.

The frequency of creating a budget is as follows:
- Monthly
- Quarterly
- Half-year (every six months; in this stage, you can do revisions)
- Annually

QuickBooks Applications

Reporting in QuickBooks

In order to do budgeting and forecasting in QuickBooks, you need to make sure that you set your fiscal year properly by understating your starting month of your fiscal year and reviewing the last fiscal year's financial reports by going to the homepage menu and running the company financial report. Based on those reports, you can make the budget or a forecast. A forecast is an actual expectation and estimate of future trends based on historical data.

Steps to Create Budget in QuickBooks

You have two options in order to create your next year's budget from scratch or use last year's P&L (profit and loss) to start a new budget.

- Go to the homepage menu and then select > Company
- Planning and budgeting > set up budgets (as shown below)
- Select: **Create new budget**
- Set the fiscal year for your budget
- Select either **P&L** or **Balance sheet** (your preference)
- Click **Next**
- If P&L is selected, you can customize (add jobs or class detail)
- Create a budget from the crutch or create budget from the previous year's actual data
- **Finish**

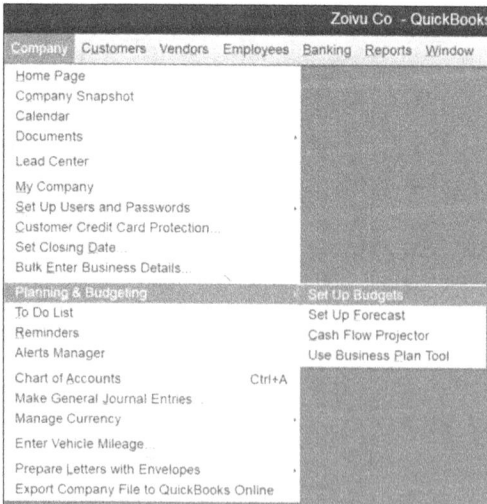

QuickBooks Applications

Reporting in QuickBooks

Steps to Create Forecasts in QuickBooks

Depending on the version of QuickBooks you are using, you can create a forecast in order to predict revenue and cash flow as well as create a financial forecast from scratch. You can also use the previous year's historical data by following these steps:

- Go to the homepage menu and then select >**Company**
- Select **Planning and budgeting**
- Set up **Forecast**
- Click on **Create new forecast**
- For the forecast, set the fiscal year and apply the same criteria same as budgeting (i.e. adding jobs and class)
- Select **Create forecast from scratch** or **create budget** from the previous year's data
- Select **finish**
- To review your budget and forecasts, go>**homepage menu**> select the **reports**>**budget and forecasts**

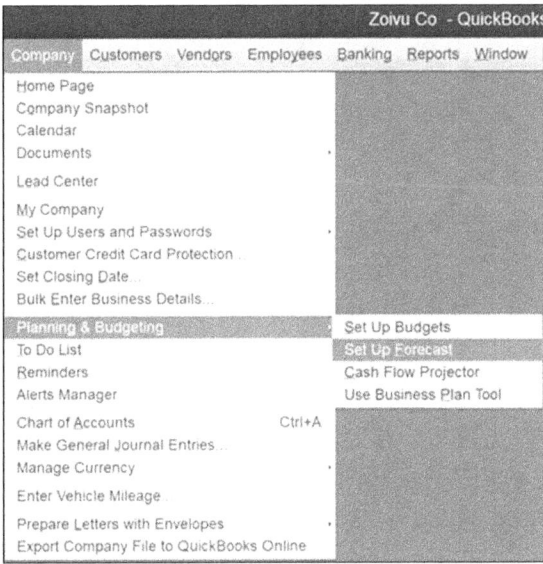

PART (III)

QuickBooks Real-World Cases

LEARNING OBJECTIVES (QUICKBOOKS CASE STUDY)

QuickBooks Case Study

Transaction in ZOIVU.CO

AS OF JANUARY 2020, THE FOLLOWING TRANSACTIONS HAPPENED IN ZOIVU CO.

Zoivu Co. is a company that is beginning to make products and provide services across the U.S. The following financial transactions occurred in the company for the beginning of the year.

The following are products and services for the company:

a) Product:
- Pen
- Notebook
- Flipchart
- Training manual

b) Services:
- Finance workshop tax
- QuickBooks workshop
- Business consultation

1. On January 2nd, there are three investors (George A., Michael B., and Charles C.), all of whom equally brought $3,000,000 each to the company as an initial investment. This yielded a total of $9,000,000, deposited in the company's checking account (ending with account 1010).

2. Owners signed an agreement between Zoivu Co. and City Lease in order to rent a building in downtown Nashville, TN, for the purpose of office location on January 2nd. A monthly lease payment of $10,500 with the condition of the first month's rent in advance was paid.

3. On January 3rd, cash withdrawal was made through writing a check #1212 by order of investors with the amount of $200,000 (from the company checking account) to Petty Cash.

4. On January 3rd, a business activity license was issued from the Department of Business and Commerce. The company charged a fee of $200 (bill #10033 to be paid within five days).

QuickBooks Case Study

Transaction in ZOIVU.CO

5. On January 3rd, some of the employees start working, and they are listed per their job tile.

6. On January 4th, the procurement started purchasing PPE – furniture and fixture for office use from the supplier IKEA. Payment was made in cash at the store for the total value of $22,200. The following items were purchased:

    - 50 office chairs at the price of $50/each (item #1050)
    - 50 office desks at the price of $85/each (item #1060)
    - 10 food tables at the price of $45/each (item #1070)
    - 100 rugs at the price of $150/each (item #1080)

7. On January 4th, they purchased 2.5 acres of land with the value of $200,000 (invoice#102030) from Land of USA. They also signed a contract with a company called Earth Construction for $350,000 (invoice 104050) to build within 25 days for the purpose of a production facility in the downtown outskirts. They agreed to pay 20% as a down payment. Both transactions were made via bank payment.

8. On January 5th, procurement made a purchase at the Machinery & Equipment on 15 days of credit with the value of $150,000 from Western Machinery Co (order #12345). It was created against the invoice #14321 from the supplier USA Machinery, which is located in Texas, for the following machines:

    - Production machine: $80,000
    - Sealing machine: $30,000
    - Heat printing machine: $20,000
    - Ink mixer machine: $20,000

Go to **list→Item List→Create above non-inventory items** and link with the fixed asset (machinery):

9. On Jan. 8, the company decided to purchase one truck and another SUV from Nissan for the purpose of office use with an equal price of $45,000 and a total value of $90,000. Nissan has shipped only two of the SUVs and tracking numbers to Zoivu Co.

QuickBooks Case Study

Transaction in ZOIVU.CO

and noted that invoices would be sent via email later.

10. On Jan. 8, Nissan sent an invoice #656540 with payment terms of Net 10 and (according to state law) 9% tax withheld.

11. On Jan. 9, there are 12 employees, and the company decided to order a computer (Microsoft Surface) for each person ($1,000 each, with a total of $12,000) from Microsoft Co. Payment was due in two partial payments on Jan. 14th and 30th for the invoice #121314.

12. On Jan. 10, **Partial Payment** to Microsoft was paid via the checking account (ending in 1010 and invoice #121314).

13. On Jan. 10, the company purchased monthly auto insurance plans for both vehicles from GEICO, which cost $1,200 for the year. They were paid in advance with an invoice #65432 and a payment was made via checking account.

14. On Jan. 12, procurement has sent a purchase order to the company B.P. Group for the following raw materials for the stock to manufacture products (including a 9% tax) with a total PO value of $158,200. The supplier has shipped the goods (invoice #556677) along with the Net 10 term.

Raw material for pen:

- a) Polystyrene   5,000 at $5/lbs.
- b) Tube and Cap   1,000,000 at $0.01/each
- c) Brass Tip   1,000,000 at $0.01/each
- d) Tungsten Carbide (a ball point) 1,000,000 at $0.01/each
- e) Ink   1,000,000 at $0.01/ounce

Raw material for notebook:

- a) Wood free writing paper   1,000,000 at $0,009/sheet
- b) Printing ink   55,000 at $0.2/liter
- c) Cover sheets   5,000,000 at $0.2/sheet
- d) Stitching wire   1,000,000 at 0.01/inch

QuickBooks Case Study

Transaction in ZOIVU.CO

Rater material for flipchart:

- a) Sheet pad   1,000,000   at $ 0.01/sheet
- b) Glue   500,000 at $0.2/liter
- c) Sticker   2,000,0000   at $0.01/each

15. On Jan. 13, the production department began manufacturing three main products, pens, notebooks, and flipcharts, 50,000 units per product using raw materials, and then putting them in stock for sale.

16. On Jan. 18, Zoivu Co. and CNBC sign a contract for 12 days' worth of product advertising and other services for $10,000. The invoice (#202526) was to be paid at the end of services.

17. On Jan. 18, the B.P. Group Supplier invoice (#556677) was paid in full via checking account (ending in 1010), as the amount was due within the Net 10 term.

18. On Jan. 20, a customer "Walmart" asked a quotation/estimate of 6,000 units of total (each 2,000). If the company accepts the quotation, the Walmart store would place an order.

19. On Jan. 20, the electricity bills arrived for $1,800 from Nashville Electricity Services (with invoice #998020), which was due by January 30th.

20. On Jan. 30, the bill was due for $1,800 to Nashville Electricity Services with invoice #998020, and the payment processes via the company's checking account (ending in 1010).

21. On Jan. 30, monthly employee salaries were processed through wire transfer from the checking account to the 12 employees' bank accounts. Salary details are shown below to be entered in the QuickBooks by making a "General Journal Entry."

22. On Jan. 30, D.C. Décor did some repair/maintenance and decoration in the office and charges for one-day services of $2,000 in check #1110 and invoice #111213.

23. On Jan. 30, 50% partial payment processes to CNBC TV for the 12 days' worth of advertisement via banking transfer from the

QuickBooks Case Study

Transaction in ZOIVU.CO

company's checking account.

24. On Jan. 31, the company processed depreciations against all fixed assets with standard usage methods.

25. On Jan. 30, the company charged a late fee on the payment to the customer.

26. The finance team decided to close the month of January on the 31st, and prior to that, they make sure to review the closing checklist in order to prevent missing any adjustment or account reconciliation. Sample of the checklist has been provided in Appendix (B).

27. On Jan. 31, the finance department decided to do the bank reconciliation and files it as a supporting document, including any necessary adjustment made.

28. On Jan.31, the end of the month/period, the board of directors asks for monthly reports to date for the following items:
    a. Monthly income statement (P&L)
    b. Balance sheet
    c. Cashflow statement
    d. Accounts Receivable
    e. Accounts Payable

QuickBooks Case Study

Real-World Example (QB)

REAL-WORLD EXAMPLE (QB)

As of January 2020, the following transactions happened in Zoivu Co.:

Zoivu Co. is a company that is beginning to make products and provide services across the U.S. The following financial transactions occurred in the company for the beginning of the year (2020).

The following are products and services for the company:
- a) Product:
    - i. Pen
    - ii. Notebook
    - iii. Flipchart
    - iv. Training manual
- b) Services:
    - i. Finance workshop tax
    - ii. QuickBooks workshop
    - iii. Business consultation

1. There are three investors (George A., Michael B., and Charles C.) who each equally brought $3,000,000 to the company as an initial investment (with a total of $9,000,000). This was deposited in the company's checking account (which ended in account#1010) on Jan. 2:

From the homepage, go to **Company**:
- a) Make general journal entries
- b) 1010 Checking BOA (**Debit**: $9,000,000)
- c) Owner's investment accounts (**Credit**: $9,000,000)
- d) Click **save & close**

QuickBooks Case Study

Real-World Example (QB)

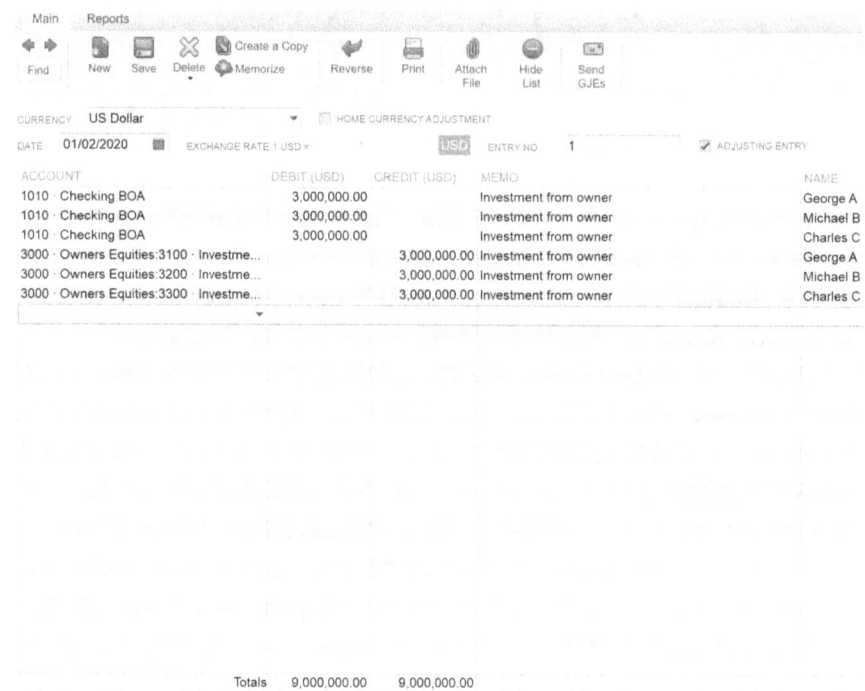

How to check the transaction posted:

2. Owners signed an agreement #01 between Zoivu Co. and City Lease in order to rent a building in downtown Nashville, TN for the purpose of office location on Jan. 2, with monthly lease payment of $10,500 (with the condition of the first month's rent in advance).

> Go to Banking:

QuickBooks Case Study

Real-World Example (QB)

- Set up vendor as **"City Lease"**
- **Write Checks**
- Select **1010 Checking BOA**
- **Select date** 01/02/2020
- **Amount**: $10,500
- Add **memo purpose of payment**
- **Order Checks** from the right corner if you want to buy the Checks
- **Save and close**

Writing Checks

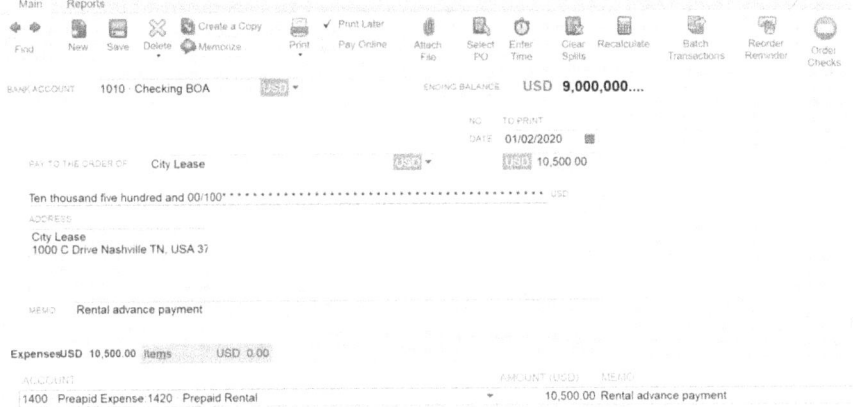

3. On Jan. 3, cash withdrawal was made through writing a check #1212 by the order of investors with the amount of $200,000 from company checking to Petty Cash.

- Go to Banking
- Transfer funds (shown below)

QuickBooks Case Study
Real-World Example (QB)

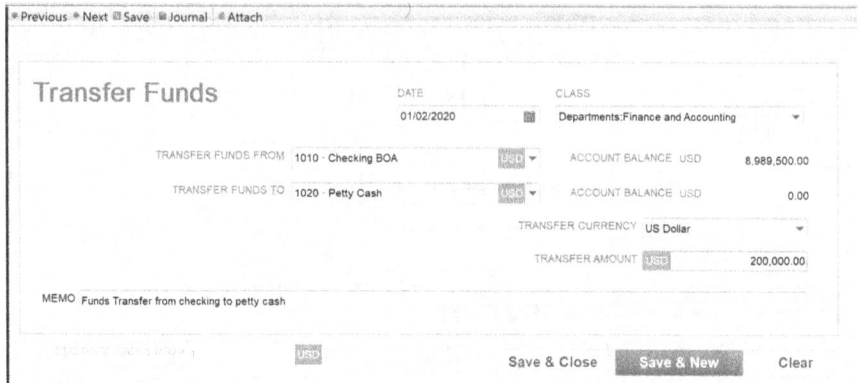

4. On Jan. 3, a business activity license has been issued from the Department of Business and Commerce. The company has charged a fee of $200,000,000,000 (#10033) to be paid within five days.

> ➢ Go to **setup vendor account** as "Department of Business and Commerce"
> ➢ **Vendors**
> ➢ Enter **Bills**
> ➢ Attach copy of invoice using "**attach file**"
> ➢ **Save and close** or **save and new** for entering another bill

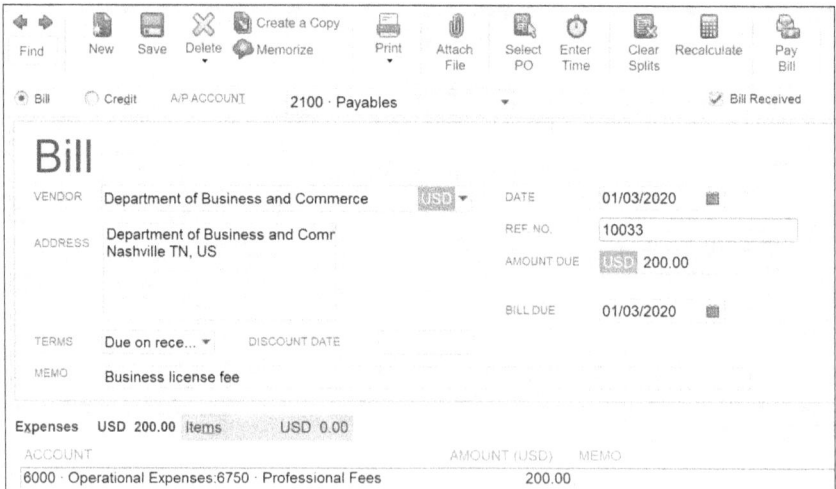

QuickBooks Case Study

Real-World Example (QB)

5. On Jan. 3, some of the employees will start working and they are listed per their job tile as the following:

Name	Title
John Abc	Chief financial officer
Charlie M	Financial analyst
Michael R	HR manager
Jacob S	Production manager
Justin J	Customer services
Tylor S	Sales representative
Samantha M	Procurement specialist
Dimond R	Finance trainer

- Go to home page → Employees
- Employee center
- New employee
- Personal information
- Address & contact
- Additional info
- Payroll info (this required to add payroll service in order to activate)
- Employment info
- Click **OK** to save

Remember the principle: The more and accurate input, the better output you will receive in QuickBooks.

QuickBooks Case Study

Real-World Example (QB)

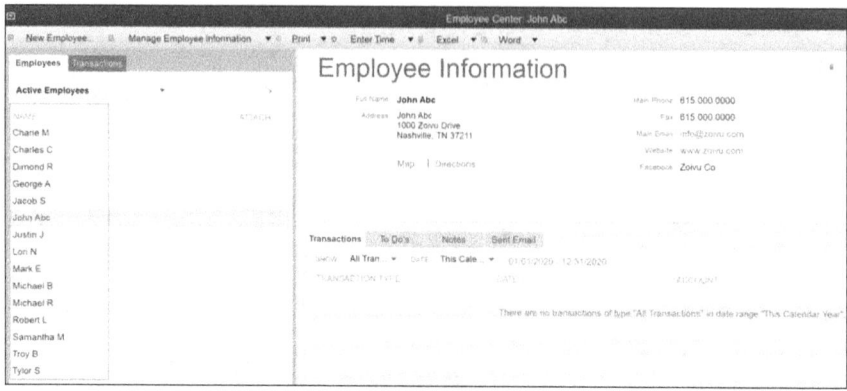

6. On Jan. 4, the procurement started purchasing PPE – furniture and fixture from supplier IKEA office use .Payment was in cash at the store for the total value of $22,200.

- 50 office Chair sat $50/each (item number 1050)
- 50 office Desk sat $85/each (item number 1060)
- 10 Food tables at $45/each (item number 1070)
- 100 Rugs at $150/each (item number 1080)

  ➢ Go to banking
  ➢ **Write Checks**
  ➢ Select "**Pay to the order of**"
  ➢ **Invoice number** (uncheck the "Print Later") and memo
  ➢ There are two option (**Expenses and Items**). Select **Item** for inventory item.
  ➢ **Item→Add new**
  ➢ **Type→Non-inventory Part>following details**
  ➢ OK

QuickBooks Case Study

Real-World Example (QB)

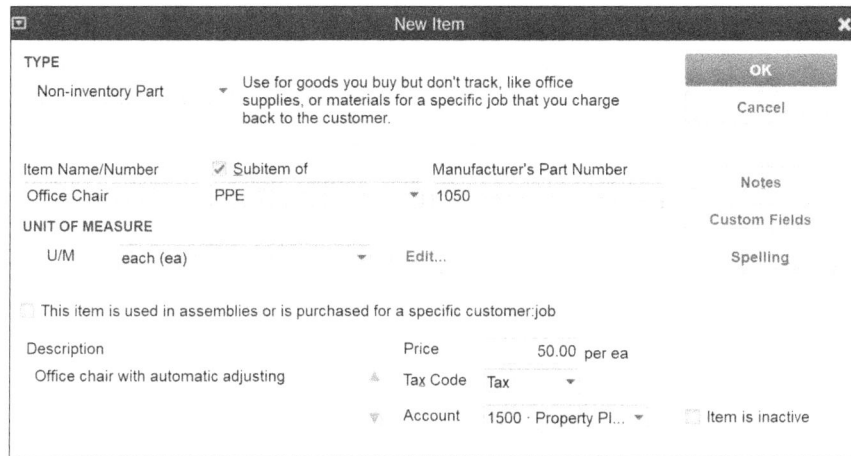

Follow the instructions below for inputting details for the purchases:

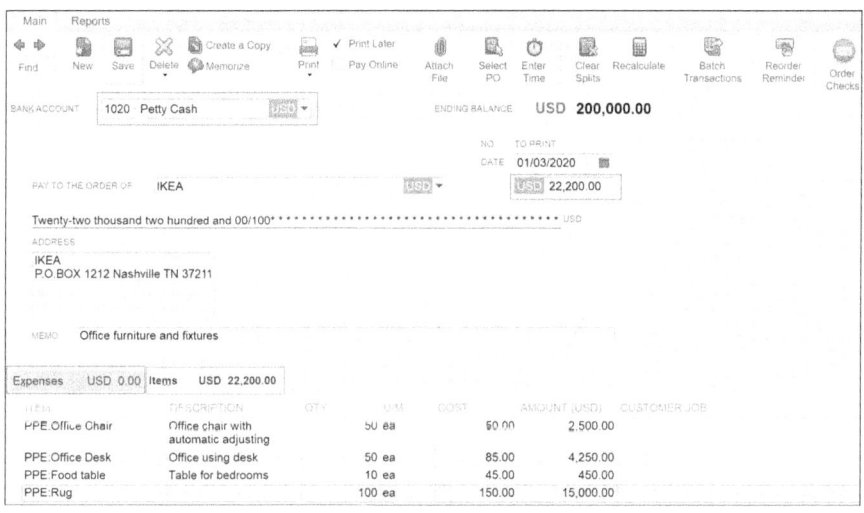

The following messages occur when posting a transaction in past date. To confirm that you still want to record in these dates, click "**Yes**." The second message alerts you that one or more items do not have assigned classes or business units(discussed in class list section). If you wish to add any, you can go back. If not, click **Save and Close**.

QuickBooks Case Study

Real-World Example (QB)

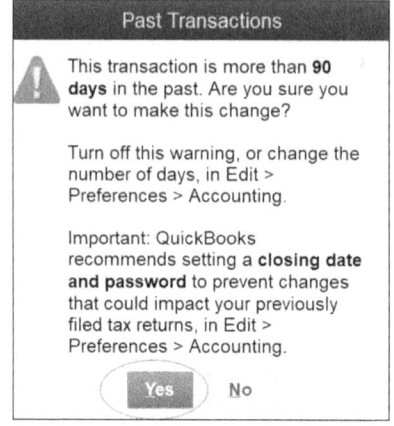
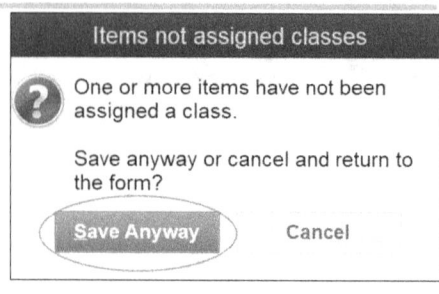

7. On Jan. 4, they purchased 2.5 acres of land with the value of $200,000 (invoice #102030) from Land of USA and signed a contract with Earth Construction for $350,000 (invoice #104050) to build a production facility in the outskirts of downtown within 25 days. They agree to pay 20% as down payment. Both transactions are made via bank payment.

- Go to Banking:
- **Write Checks→** 1010 Checking BOA
- **Pay to the order of→Add New→Vendor** (Land of USA, Earth Construction)
- Once the following information entered, click "**save and close**"

QuickBooks Case Study
Real-World Example (QB)

➢ Set up new vendor as **"Earth Construction"**
➢ **Home page→Vendor→Enter Bills**
➢ **Attach the copy of invoice**
➢ **Save and close**

See details in the following image:

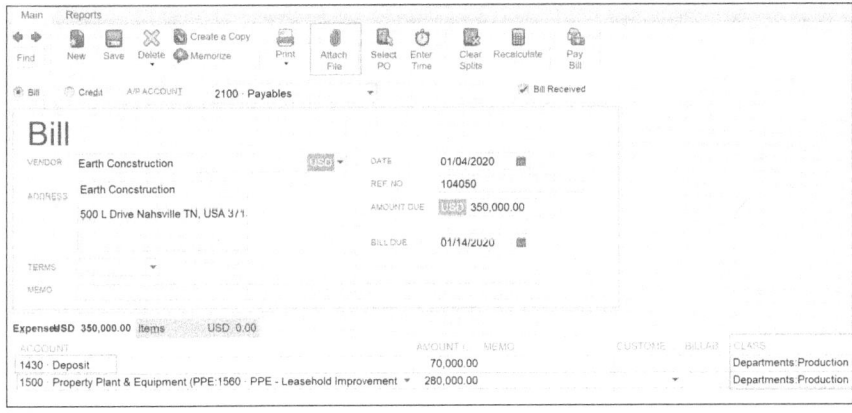

QuickBooks Case Study

Real-World Example (QB)

8. On Jan. 5, procurement made a purchase from Machinery & Equipment on 15 days credit with the value of $150,000 from Western Machinery Co. (order #12345) created for the invoice #14321, from the supplier USA Machinery located in Texas for the following machines:

- Production machine: $80,000
- Sealing machine: $30,000
- Heat printing machine: $20,000
- Ink mixer machine: $20,000

> Go list→item list→create above non-inventory items and link with fixed asset (machinery):
>
> Setup vendor as "USA Machinery "→vendor
>
> Crate purchase orders (PO)
>
> Image below shows the PO details:

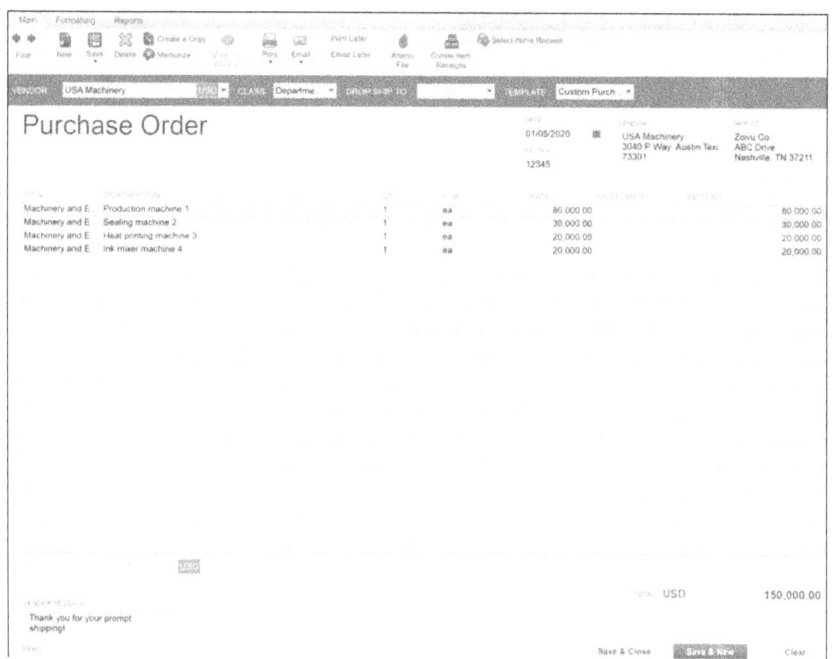

QuickBooks Case Study

Real-World Example (QB)

The following image shows how PO looks in print preview as **print and mail** or **save it as a PDF** (and email instead). You can always edit and change to your preference, as well as add a logo on your PO/Invoice.

Zoivu Co
ABC Drive
Nashville, TN 37211

Purchase Order

Date	P.O. No.
1/5/2020	12345

Vendor	Ship To
USA Machinery 3040 P Way Austin Texas, USA 73301	Zoivu Co ABC Drive Nashville, TN 37211

Item	Description	Qty	U/M	Rate	Amount
Production mac...	Production machine 1	1	ea	80,000.00	80,000.00
Sealing machine	Sealing machine 2	1	ea	30,000.00	30,000.00
Heat printing m...	Heat printing machine 3	1	ea	20,000.00	20,000.00
Ink mixer machi...	Ink mixer machine 4	1	ea	20,000.00	20,000.00

Thank you for your prompt shipping!

Total USD 150,000.00

QuickBooks Case Study

Real-World Example (QB)

The supplier shipped the goods along with the invoice for payment. You can automatically change existing PO to invoice and receive items through the following process:

- ➤ Home page → Vendors
- ➤ Received Items and Enter Bill
- ➤ Select vendor for this as "**USA Machinery**"
- ➤ The following message pops up:

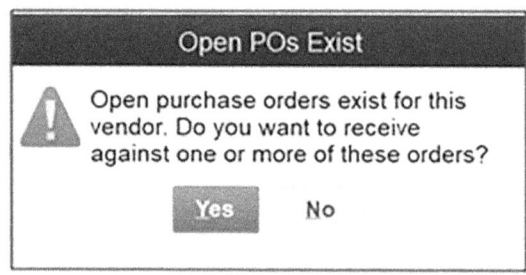

- ➤ Click "Yes"
- ➤ Tick the following date circled as red color and then click "OK"

Once you have selected it and clicked OK, the next page will pop-up that drops all item details from existing PO into a Bill format that is ready to be invoiced. You can check and compare them with the PO, as well as items that were physically received to make sure you have everything you ordered. You can contact the vendor for justifications if there are any discrepancies (i.e. the bill does not match with the PO). Enter the invoice number (14321) as mentioned above and other details such as a memo, or terms of payment and invoice date.

QuickBooks Case Study

Real-World Example (QB)

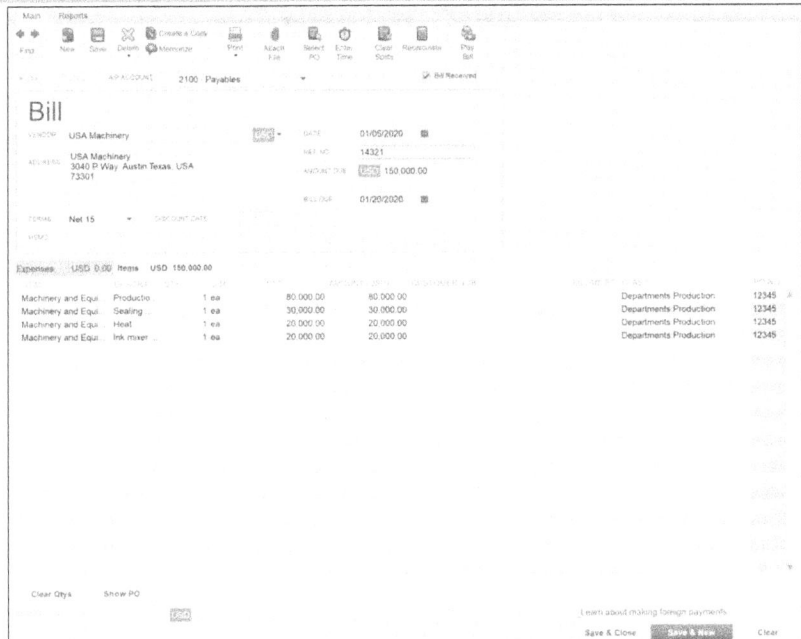

You can use different methods depending on how and when you are receiving the goods. If you received the goods only but no invoice, at this point, you can just select "Item Received." Also, in case you have received the item already (and the bill arrives later), then select "Enter Bill for Received Items."

Note: At some point, if you get the message below, this means that you're entering transactions from the past date. To confirm, you can click "Yes," or if it happened by mistake, click "No" and correct the date.

QuickBooks Case Study

Real-World Example (QB)

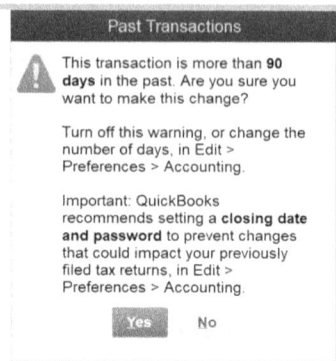

9. On Jan. 5, the owner asked for account payables report balance details in order to get an idea of how much money we owe units this period. The Financial Analyst generates the AP report as the following steps:

   ➤ Home page > Reports
   ➤ Vendors & Payables
   ➤ Vendor Balance Details

Zoivu Co
Vendor Balance Detail
All Transactions

Type	Date	Num	Account	Amount	Balance
Department of Business and Commerce					
Bill	01/03/2020	10033	2100 · Payables	200.00	200.00
Total Department of Business and Commerce				200.00	200.00
Earth Concstruction					
Bill	01/04/2020	104050	2100 · Payables	350,000.00	350,000.00
Total Earth Concstruction				350,000.00	350,000.00
USA Machinery					
Bill	01/05/2020	14321	2100 · Payables	150,000.00	150,000.00
Total USA Machinery				150,000.00	150,000.00
TOTAL				500,200.00	500,200.00

10. On Jan. 8, the company decides to purchase one truck and another SUV from Nissan for the purpose of office use at the price of $45,000 each and total value of $90,000.
    - Nissan has shipped only two of the vehicle's SUV and tracking number to Zoivu Co. and noted that invoices will be sent via email later.

      ➤ Go to homepage and Vendor
      ➤ Receive Items
      ➤ Input good received note details "GRN"

QuickBooks Case Study
Real-World Example (QB)

➢ Save and close. See details exhibited below:

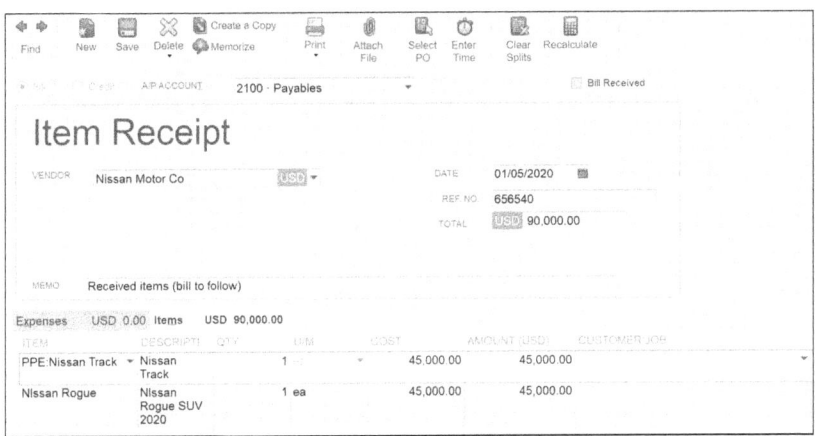

11. On Jan. 8, Nissan has sent an invoice #656540 with payment terms of Net 10 and (according to state law) 9% tax withheld.

    ➢ Go to homepage > Vendor

    ➢ Enter Bill for Received Items

    ➢ New page pops up > select Vendor as "Nissan Motor Co."

    ➢ Tick the "Use item receipt date for the bill date"

    ➢ Click OK

QuickBooks Case Study

Real-World Example (QB)

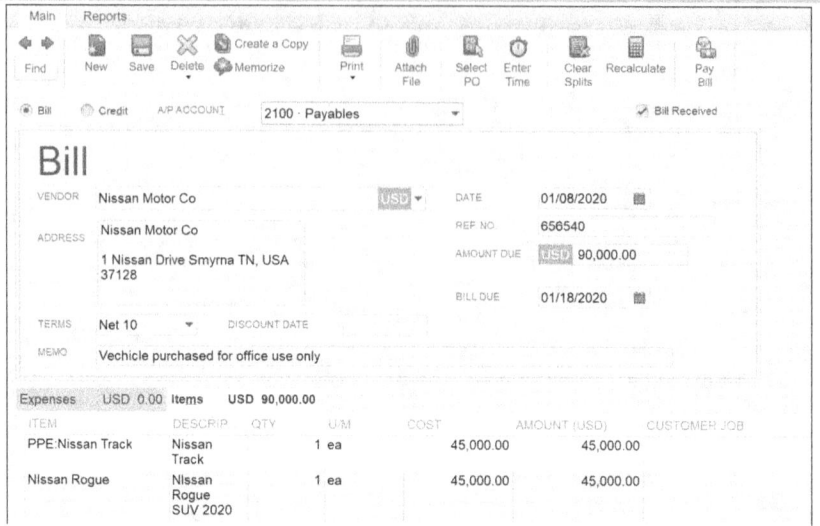

12. On Jan. 9, there are 12 employees in the company. They decide to order a computer (Microsoft Surface) for each employee at $1,000 each (total: $12,000) from Microsoft Co. Payment is due into two partial payments on January 14th and 30th for the invoice number 121314.

> ➢ Go to Vendors → Vendor center and set up new account as "Microsoft Co."
> ➢ List → Add new item list → Non-inventory item
> ➢ Sub-account of PPE- computer and equipment
> ➢ Go back to Vendors →**Received Item and Enter Bill**
> ➢ Enter the following details →**Save and close**

QuickBooks Case Study
Real-World Example (QB)

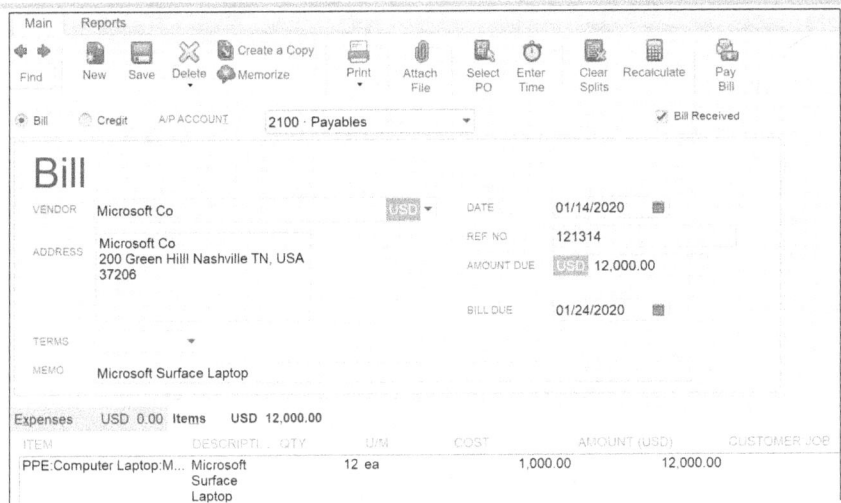

13. On Jan. 10, **Partial Payment** of Microsoft is paid via BOA checking account (ending in 1010) and invoice number 121314.

> - Go to Vendors
> - Pay Bills
> - Tick only Microsoft Co.→ Change amount to pay from $12,000 to $6,000
> - Select account 1010 checking BOA as mentioned above
> - Click "**Pay Selected Bills**"
> - Print check

QuickBooks Case Study

Real-World Example (QB)

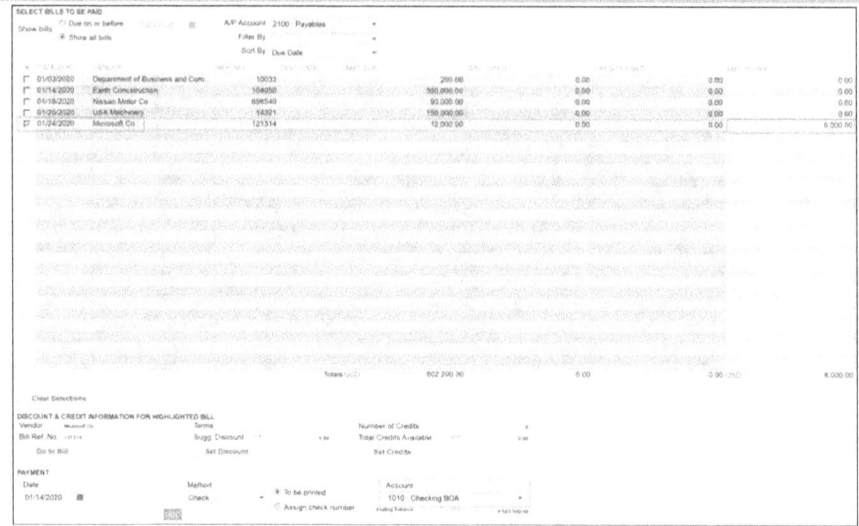

14. On Jan. 10, the company has purchased a monthly auto insurance plan for both vehicles from GEICO that cost $1,200 for the whole year. It was paid in advance via checking account with invoice number 65432.

Step one

➢ Home page → Vendors → Setup new account as "GEICO"

➢ Enter Bill

➢ Enter the details as the following →**save and close**

QuickBooks Case Study

Real-World Example (QB)

Step two:

- ➢ Go back to **Vendors**
- ➢ Pay Bills
- ➢ Select or filter by specific vendor "GEICO"
- ➢ Make sure bank and date are correct
- ➢ Click "**Pay Selected Bills**"
- ➢ Check report or GJ to ensure that the transaction was made correctly

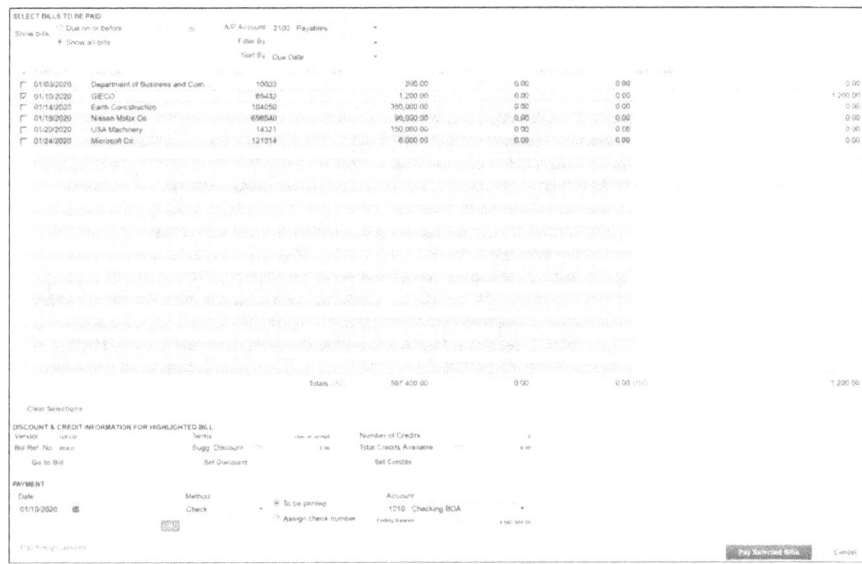

In the following image, you can "Print Checks." If not paying via check, click "Done."

QuickBooks Case Study

Real-World Example (QB)

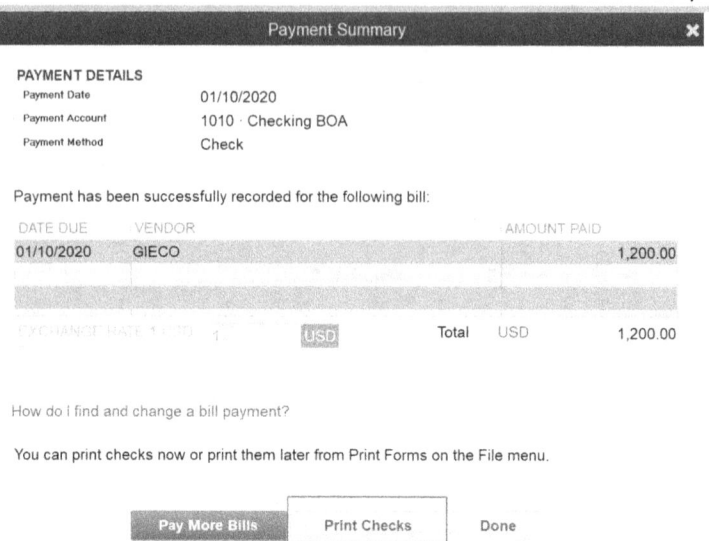

15. On Jan. 12, procurement has sent a purchase order to the company BP Group for the following raw materials for the stock to manufacture products (including 9% tax) with total PO value of $158,200. The supplier has shipped the goods along with the invoice number 556677, Net 10 term.

Raw materials for pen:

- Polystyrene   5,000 at $5.00/lbs.
- Tube and cap   1,000,000 at $0.01/each
- Brass Tip   1,000,000 at $0.01/each
- Tungsten carbide- a ball point   1,000,000 at $0.01/each
- Ink   1,000,000 at $0.01/ounce

Raw materials for notebook:

- Wood free writing paper 1,000,000 at $0.09/sheet
- Printing ink   55,000 at $0.2/liter
- Cover sheets   5,000,000 at $0.2/sheet
- Stitching wire   1,000,000 at 0.01/inch

Rater materials for flipchart:

QuickBooks Case Study

Real-World Example (QB)

- Sheet pad   1,000,000 at $0.01/sheet
- Glue   500,000 at $0.2/liter
- Sticker   2,000,0000 at $0.01/each

Step One:
- Vendors → Create Purchase Order
- Setup new vendor account as **"BP Group"**
- Enter details as exhibited on the following page
- Print the PO or email directly to the supplier. You can save as PDF and email it later after it is physically signed and stamped.
- Save and close

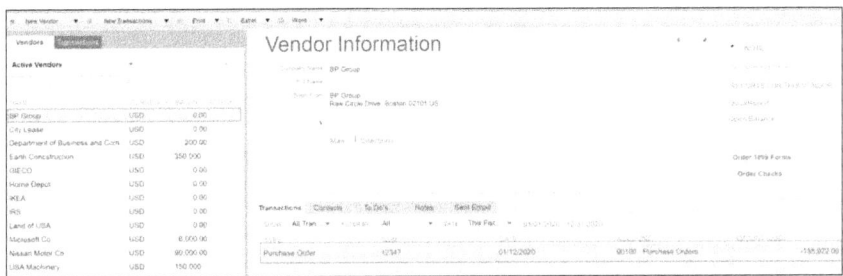

Look at the vendor center below to see the transaction details and activity for each vendor listed. (Ex. BP Group)

Step Two: Check the status of inventory before receiving goods
- Go to Reports
- Inventory
- Inventory Stock Status by Item → See exhibited below before receiving goods

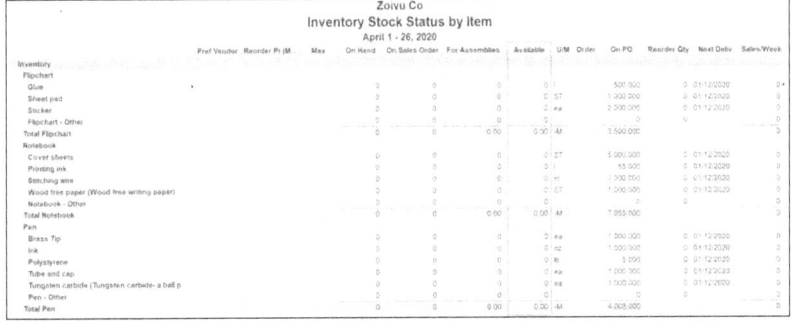

QuickBooks Case Study

Real-World Example (QB)

Step Three:

Go to homepage and Vendors
- Receive Items and Enter Bill
- Select the open purchase orders and press left side of the date to "tick mark"
- Click OK
- All data is dropped from the existing PO into a Bill. Review them for accuracy.
- (See image below)
- Enter invoice number as 556677, term Net 10, and memo, then save and close.

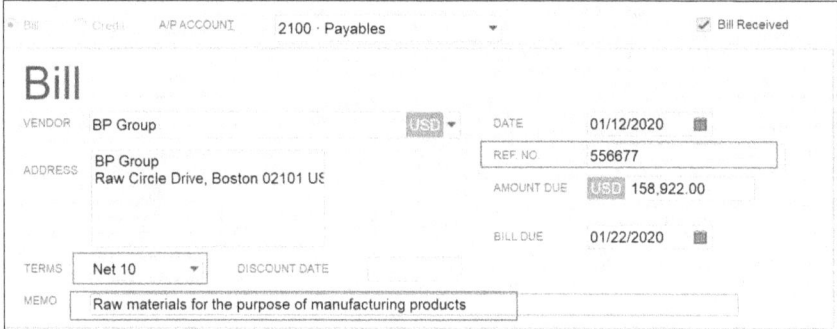

Step Four: Check the status of inventory after receiving goods
- Go to Reports
- Inventory
- Inventory Stock Status by Item > See image below before receiving goods
- Compare this step with step two for changes (exhibited below):

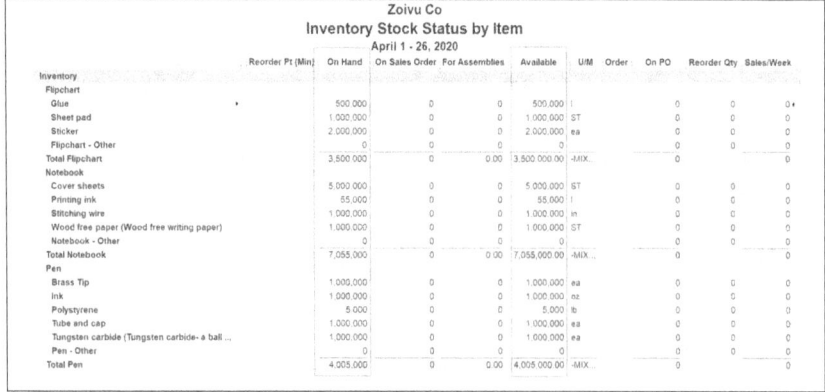

QuickBooks Case Study
Real-World Example (QB)

On Jan. 13, the production department has started to manufacture three main products such as Pen, Notebook, and Flipchart (each 50,000 units) using raw materials. They put them in stock for sale.

Step One:
- From the homepage menu → Vendors
- Inventory and activities
- Build assemblies
- Assembly Item → Add new → "Pen"
- Inventory assembly
- Here is the product formulation (Enter the name of products intend to manufacture):

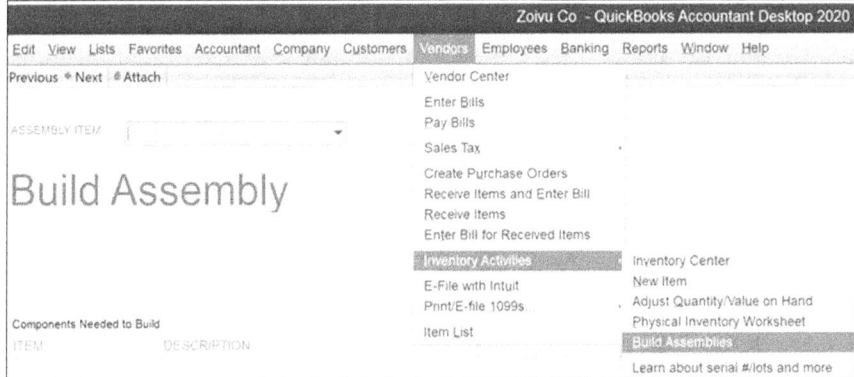

Step Two: For example, Zoivu Co. wants to produce the following three products:

    i. Pen

    ii. Notebook

    iii. Flipchart

QuickBooks Case Study

Real-World Example (QB)

In the new item page below, enter all information and formulate the way you want for each product:

Pen (I):

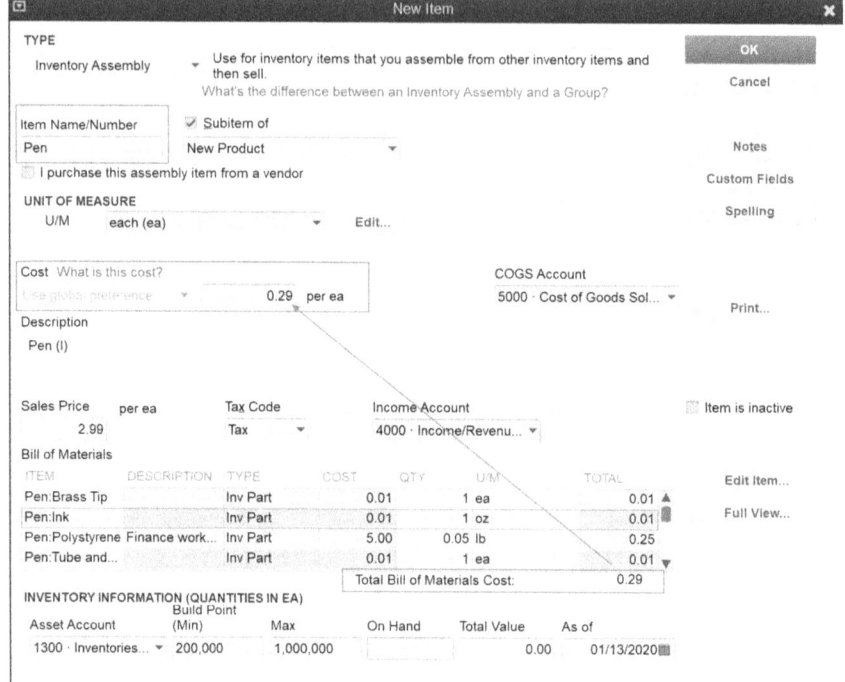

Note: Make sure to select account 1300... Work – In_ Progress (WIP)

QuickBooks Case Study

Real-World Example (QB)

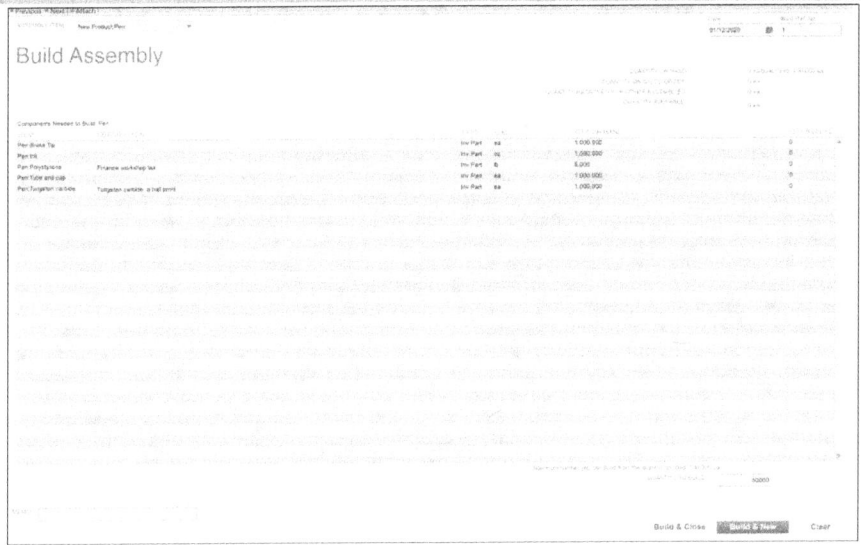

Notebook (II): Follow the same steps as (I) used for producing Pen
From the homepage menu → Vendors

- Inventory and activities
- Build assemblies
- Assembly Item → Add new → "Notebook"
- Inventory assembly
- Below is the product formulation (enter the name of products intended to manufacture)

QuickBooks Case Study

Real-World Example (QB)

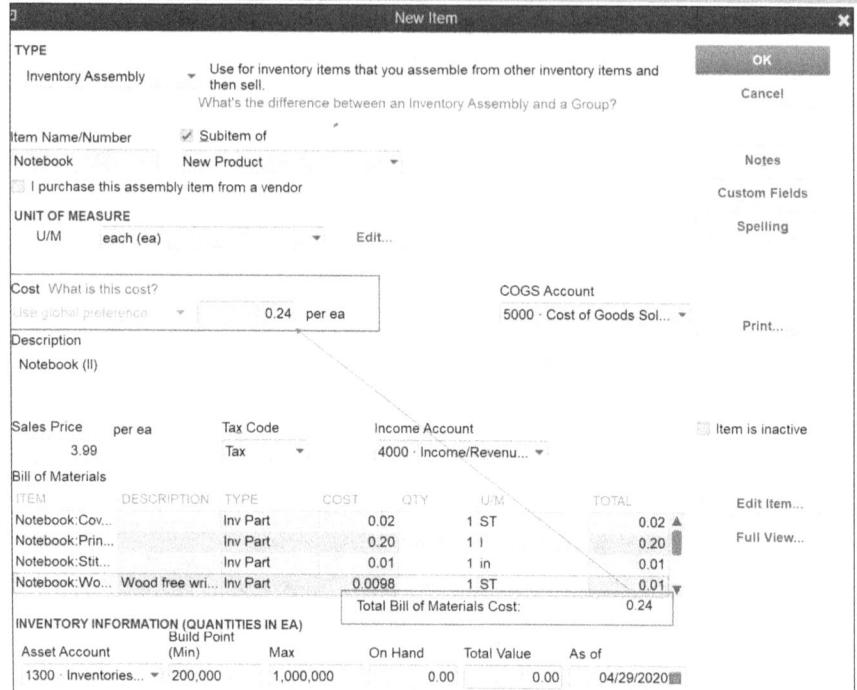

Flipchart (III): Follow the same steps as (I & II) for producing Pen & Notebook

- From the homepage menu → Vendors
- Inventory and activities
- Build assemblies
- Assembly Item → Add new → "Flipchart"
- Inventory assembly
- Below is the product formulation (enter the name of products intended to manufacture

QuickBooks Case Study

Real-World Example (QB)

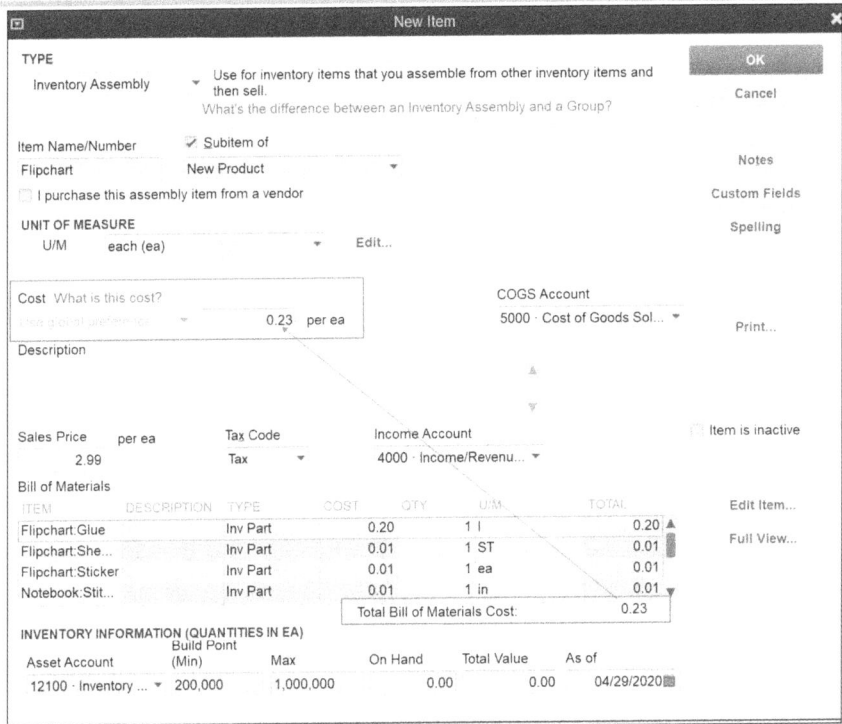

If you check the status of inventory after production (Built Assembly), then compare it with the earlier report, there is a new product added as indicated below:

- Go to Reports
- Inventory
- Inventory Stock Status by Item → See exhibited below before receiving goods

QuickBooks Case Study

Real-World Example (QB)

Compare this step with step "two." Changes are shown below:

Zoivu Co
Inventory Stock Status by Item
April 1 - 29, 2020

Inventory	Pref Vendor	Reorder Pt (Min)	Max	On Hand	On Sales Order	For Assemblies	Available	U/M	Order	On PO	Reorder Qty
Flipchart											
Glue				450.000	0	0	450.000	l		0	0
Sheet pad				950.000	0	0	950.000	ST		0	0
Sticker				1,950.000	0	0	1,950.000	ea		0	0
Flipchart - Other				0	0	0	0			0	0
Total Flipchart				3,350.000	0	0.00	***** **	-M-		0	
Notebook											
Cover sheets				4,950.000	0	0	4,950.000	ST		0	0
Printing ink				5.000	0	0	5.000	l		0	0
Stitching wire				900.000	0	0	900.000	in		0	0
Wood free paper (Wood free writing paper)				950.000	0	0	950.000	ST		0	0
Notebook - Other				0	0	0	0			0	0
Total Notebook				6,805.000	0	0.00	***** **	-M-		0	
Pen											
Brass Tip				950.000	0	0	950.000	ea		0	0
Ink				950.000	0	0	950.000	oz		0	0
Polystyrene				2.500	0	0	2.500	lb		0	0
Tube and cap				950.000	0	0	950.000	ea		0	0
Tungsten carbide (Tungsten carbide- a ball po...				950.000	0	0	950.000	ea		0	0
Pen - Other				0	0	0	0			0	0
Total Pen				3,802.500	0	0.00	***** **	-M-		0	
Assembly											
New Product											
Flipchart		200.000	1,000.000	50.000	0	0	50.000	ea	↙	0	950.000
Notebook (Notebook (N))		200.000	1,000.000	50.000	0	0	50.000	ea	↙	0	950.000
Pen (Pen (I))		200.000	1,000.000	50.000	0	0	50.000	ea	↙	0	950.000
New Product - Other				0	0	0	0			0	0
Total New Product				150.000	0	0.00	150,000.00	ea		0	

16. On Jan.18, Zoivu Co. and CNBC signed a contract for 12 days' worth of product advertising and services for $10,000. Invoice#202526 was to be paid at the end of services.

To set this up, follow the next steps:

- ➢ Advertisement Expense→Set up new vendor account as "CNBC TV"
- ➢ Homepage menu → Vendor Center
- ➢ Create new vendor account as mentioned above
- ➢ Vendors → Enter Bills in order to create an invoice to keep up with the payment
- ➢ Terms → Add new terms "Net 12" → then click "Ok"
- ➢ Enter the date, invoice number, $ amount, and description
- ➢ Expense → select the 6010 expense (advertising exp account)
- ➢ Enter a description that best describes your transaction ("TV advertisement")

QuickBooks Case Study
Real-World Example (QB)

See details below:

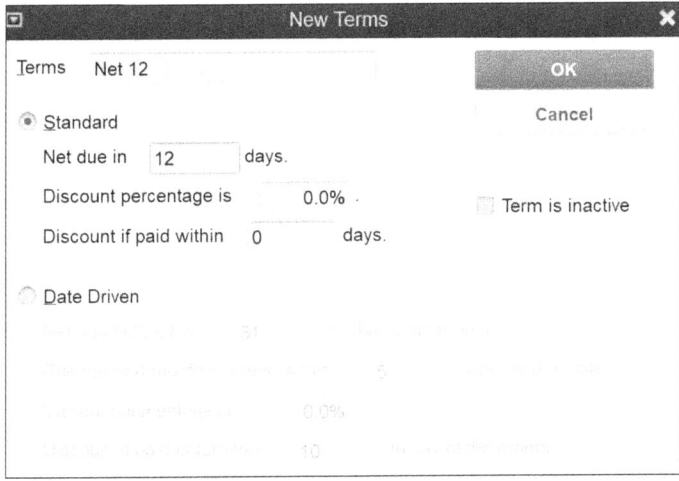

17. On Jan. 18, the BP Group Supplier (invoice number 556677) paid in full via checking account (ending in 1010) as the amount was due within Net 10 term.

Before paying bills, let's look at the Balance Sheet and payment bills that will significantly impact reduction to the account payables and liability side.

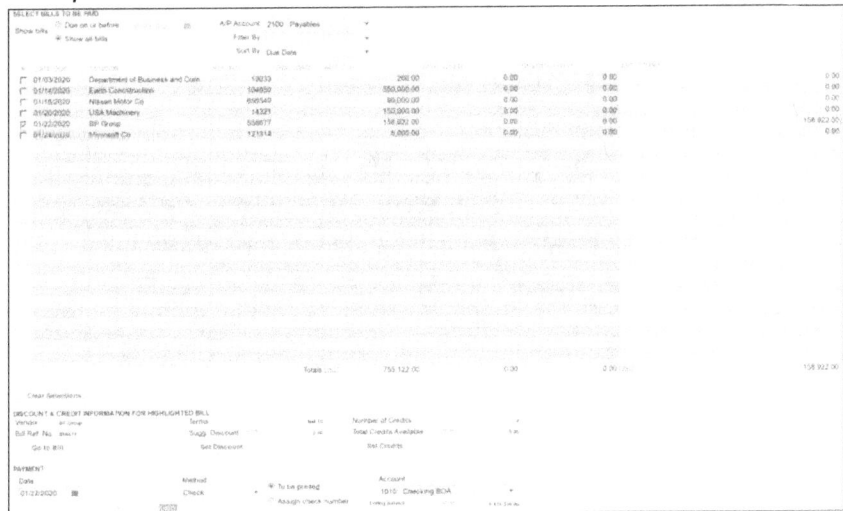

QuickBooks Case Study

Real-World Example (QB)

Follow these steps to pay the bills:
- Go to vendors
- **Pay Bills**
- Select the vendor you wish to pay (i.e. "BP Group")
- Check the banking and select appropriately
- Click the green button **"Pay Selected Bills"**
- Ensure that the AP report and BP Group balance is zero

18. On Jan. 20, a customer "Walmart" asked the company for a quotation/estimate for 6,000 units in total (each 2,000). If they accepted the quotation, the Walmart store would place an order.

Step one:
- Go to customer center > Add new customer
- Customer→create estimate→select class as **"Sales Department"**
- Select the correct date, estimate number "100200"
- **Item→** Under New Product (Pen, Notebook and Flipchart"
- **Q**uantity(2,000 each) and the rest fills in automatically
- You can customize messages like "Thank you for your business"
- Add an additional note (optional)→ select tax if applicable →Sign, scan, and send the estimate →**save and close** or **cancel** if you do not wish to continue

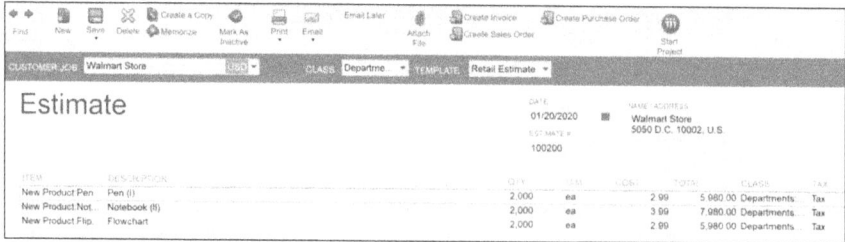

QuickBooks Case Study

Real-World Example (QB)

Step two: 6,000 units of products were sold to retailer "Walmart" at selling price already specified. They would pay within the next 10 days via bank transfer to the checking account (ending in 1010). Invoice number is 400500.

- Go to Setup new Customer Account as "Walmart"
- Go to Customer → Create invoices

Once you select the customer, the estimate will automatically pop up so you can directly convert to invoice. Shows as "**Available Estimates**" (see exhibited below):

- Click the "OK" button. It gives you different options, such as the following:
- If you want to create an invoice for the entire estimate (100%)
- If you want to create an invoice for a percentage of the entire estimate
- If you want to create an invoice for the selected item or different percentages of each item

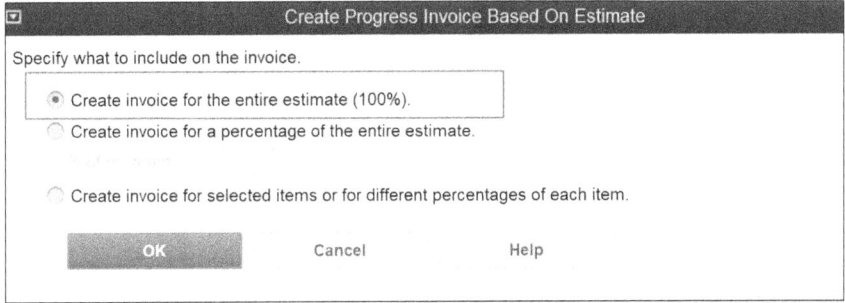

QuickBooks Case Study
Real-World Example (QB)

a) Since we want the entire invoice details to be imported, see the figure below:

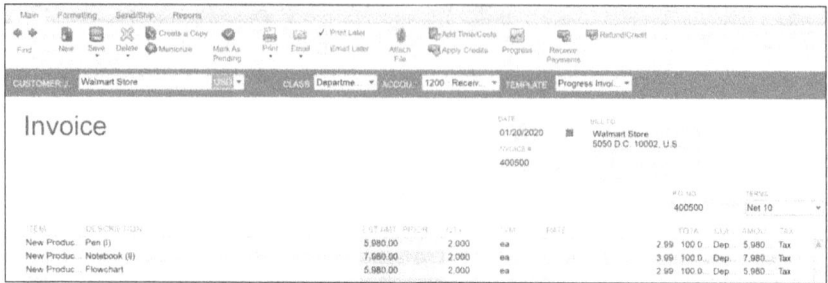

b) **Save & new** or clear (in case you don't wish to process the current invoice)

Take the following steps to see the effect in (P&L) or an income statement:

➢ From the homepage menu go to →**Reports**

➢ **Company & Financial**

➢ **Profit & Loss Standard** → from **Date**, select all and refresh

➢ If you see the total revenues of $19,9140 generated and the same thing COGS as direct cost associated with the products increased as well for $1,123.60.

QuickBooks Case Study

Real-World Example (QB)

Now, take the following steps to see the effect in (P&L) or income statement:

- From homepage menu go to > Reports
- Company & Financial
- Profit & Loss Standard > from Date, select all and refresh
- The total revenue of $19,9140 was generated, which was the same amount for COGS. Direct cost associated with the products increased at $1,123.60.

Zoivu Co
Profit & Loss
All Transactions

Jan 30, 20

Income	
4000 · Income/Revenue	
4010 · Sales of Pen	5,980.00
4020 · Sales of Notebook	7,980.00
4030 · Sales Flipchart	5,980.00
Total 4000 · Income/Revenue	19,940.00
Total Income	**19,940.00**
Cost of Goods Sold	
5000 · Cost of Goods Sold (COGS)	
5010 · COGS of Pen	580.00
5020 · COGS of Notebook	443.60
5030 · COGS of Flipchart	100.00
Total 5000 · Cost of Goods Sold (CO...	1,123.60
Total COGS	**1,123.60**
Gross Profit	**18,816.40**
Expense	
6000 · Operational Expenses	
6010 · Advertising Expense	10,000.00
6750 · Professional Fees	200.00
7000 · Payroll Taxes	14,253.00
7250 · Repairs Expense	2,000.00
7300 · Salaries Expense	31,752.00
7500 · Utilities Expense	1,800.00
Total 6000 · Operational Expenses	60,005.00
8000 · TN Tax 9%	13,122.00
Total Expense	**73,127.00**
Net Income	**-54,310.60**

To investigate what happened on the inventory side as Zoivu Co. sold 6,000 units of its products to Walmart:

- ➢ Go to homepage menu
- ➢ Reports → Inventory
- ➢ Inventory Stock Status by Items
- ➢ 50,000 units were products for each item in stock. The chart below shows 48,000 for each as the 2,000 were sold to Walmart. If you double click on each item, it will show you the details or deduction result.

QuickBooks Case Study

Real-World Example (QB)

19. On Jan. 20, the electricity bills arrive for $1,800 from Nashville Electricity Services with the invoice number 998020, which is due by January 30th.

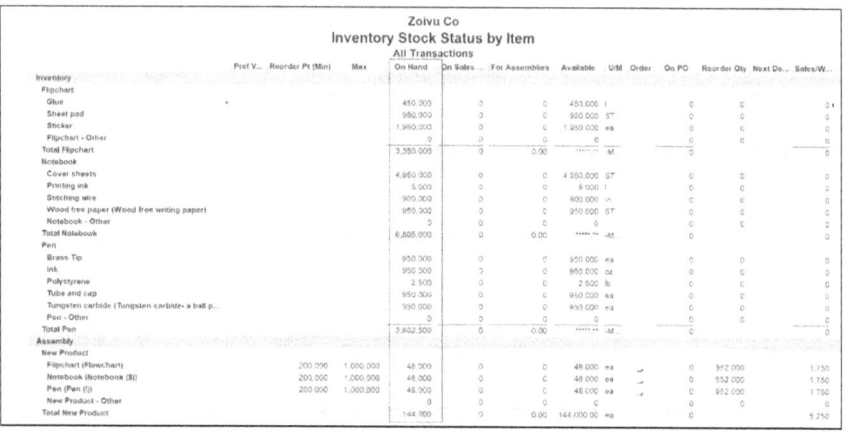

- Since paying electricity is a utility expense, follow the steps below:

    ➢ **Vendors**

    ➢ **Enter Bills**

    ➢ Select vendor "Nashville Electricity Services." If it doesn't exist already, **Add new**

    ➢ Add Invoice date, invoice number, amount, terms of payment, and description

    ➢ **Save and close**

QuickBooks Case Study

Real-World Example (QB)

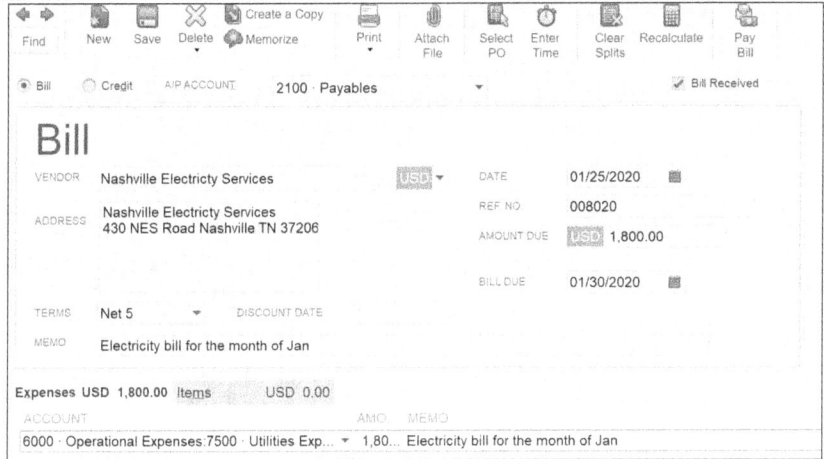

20. On Jan. 30, the bill was due for $1,800 to Nashville Electricity Services with the invoice number 998020, and the payment processes via the company's checking account (ending in 1010).

> Vendors

> Pay Bills → Select any specific vendor to pay (i.e. "Nashville Electricity Services")

> Pay Selected Bills

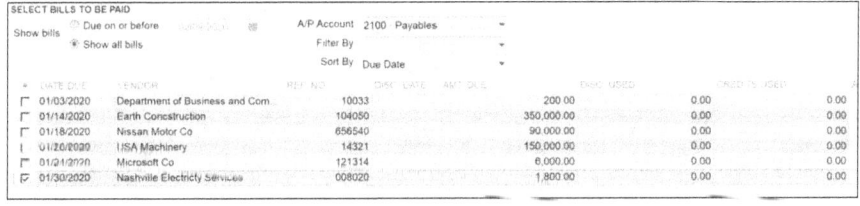

QuickBooks Case Study

Real-World Example (QB)

21. On Jan. 30, monthly employee salaries were processed through wire transfer from the checking account to their 12 employees' bank accounts. Salary details are shown below to be entered in QuickBooks by making a "General Journal Entry":

The started date for all employees considered in January 3rd, 2020

Name	Title	M Salary	Tax	Net Pay
John Abc	CFO	$ 6,000	$ 2,020	$ 3,980
Charlies M	Financial Analyst	$ 4,000	$ 1,224	$ 2,776
Michael R	HR Manager	$ 4,000	$ 1,224	$ 2,776
Jacob S	Production Manager	$ 4,000	$ 1,224	$ 2,776
Justin J	Customer Services	$ 3,000	$ 910	$ 2,090
Tylor S	Sales Representative	$ 3,500	$ 1,067	$ 2,433
Samantha M	Procurement Specialist	$ 4,000	$ 1,224	$ 2,776
Dimond R	Finance Trainer	$ 4,500	$ 1,406	$ 3,094
Mark E	Business Consultant	$ 3,000	$ 910	$ 2,090
Robert L	Tax Consultant	$ 3,000	$ 910	$ 2,090
Lori N	Production LB 1	$ 4,000	$ 1,224	$ 2,776
Troy B	Production LB 2	$ 3,000	$ 910	$ 2,090
Total Monthly Salary + Tax		$46,005	$14,253	$31,752

To make a Journal Entry, go to "Company":
- ➤ **Make General Journal** Entries
- ➤ Select the **currency "USD,"** enter **date, number or invoice number** "2," and other details
- ➤ **Save and close**

QuickBooks Case Study

Real-World Example (QB)

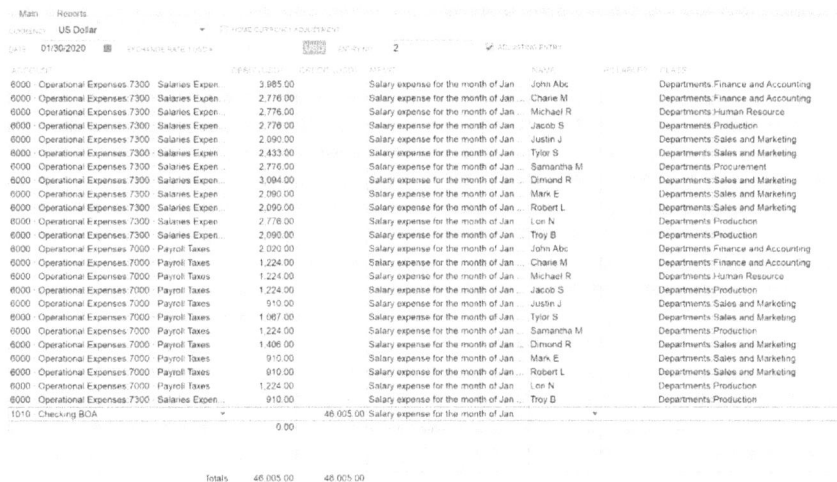

Another way to enter salary expenses is to import the IIF file into QuickBooks directly. It is entirely optional and up to you which method you use.

22. On Jan. 30, a D.C. Décor did some repair, maintenance, and decoration in the office and charged for one day's worth of services of $2,000 in check #1110 and invoice #111213

> - This is in **expense charges**→ Banking
> - **Write Checks**
> - **Add new vendor** as "D.C. Décor"
> - Enter the details as the following exhibition below
> - **Save and close**, **save and new** or clear (if you do not wish to record this entry)

QuickBooks Case Study

Real-World Example (QB)

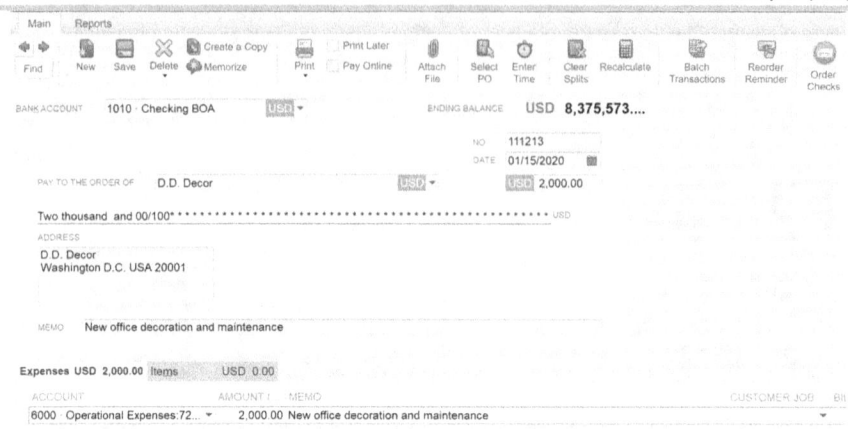

23. On Jan. 30, 50% partial payment was processed to CNBC TV for the 12 days' worth of advertisement via banking transfer from the company's checking account.

To process payments:

> ➢ Go to **Vendors→Pay Bills**
> ➢ Select CNBC TV from all other vendor list
> ➢ From **"AMT. TO Pay"** column, edit the amount from $10,000 to $5,000 that contains only 50% partial payment
> ➢ Review information →**OK**→ **"Pay Selected Bills"**

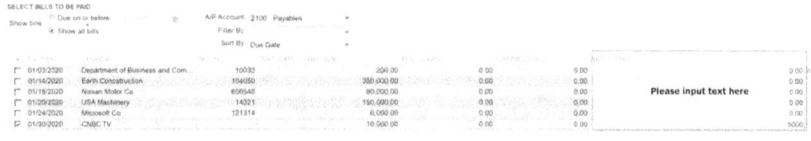

24. On Jan. 31, the company processed depreciations against all fixed assets with the standard usage method.

There are two ways you can list fixed assets and run depreciation on a monthly basis:

1. **Manually:** You can simply do all calculation and valuation utilizing Excel and imports in QuickBooks

2. **Automatically:** This way, you should consider activating the "Fixed Asset" feature option in QuickBooks, which separates work-advanced, based fixed asset in QB.

QuickBooks Case Study

Real-World Example (QB)

In order to know how to run the depreciation and enter in appropriate accounts in QuickBooks, we just need to follow the first step (which is the basic manual option):

If you look at the Balance Sheet which contains (Asset = Liabilities + Owner's equity), you will already realize that we have recorded six different types of fixed asset under the "Fixed Asset" and Property Plant and Equipment (PPE) category. These are the following:

- Building
- Machinery & Equipment
- Vehicles
- Computer and Equipment
- Furniture and Fixture
- Leasehold Improvement (Non-Depreciable)

Now, you can simply see the balance sheet report and get the data and fixed asset list details such as asset name, date of purchase, value, useful life, residual or salvage value, etc.

Asset Name	Cost/Value	Year	Salvage	UL	Method	2020 YTD Cost	Monthly Cost
Building	200,000	2020	500	6	SL	33,250	2,771
Machinery & Equipment	150,000	2020	500	6	SL	24,917	2,076
Vehicles	90,000	2020	500	5	SL	17,900	1,492
Computer and Equipment	12,000	2020	500	5	SL	2,300	192
Furniture & Fixture	22,200	2020	500	5	SL	4,340	362
Total Annual/Monthly Depreciation Expense (USD)						$ 82,707	$ 6,893

Since we have information about the annual and monthly depreciation cost, we make a "Journal Entry" as the following example for building (and the same thing can be applied to all).

1. Depreciation expenses 6,350 "Debit" for the building used code from the chart of account and amount $2,771. Accumulated Depreciation: 1610 "Credit" (the same amount: $2,771) and apply class depending upon which department used the asset.

QuickBooks Case Study

Real-World Example (QB)

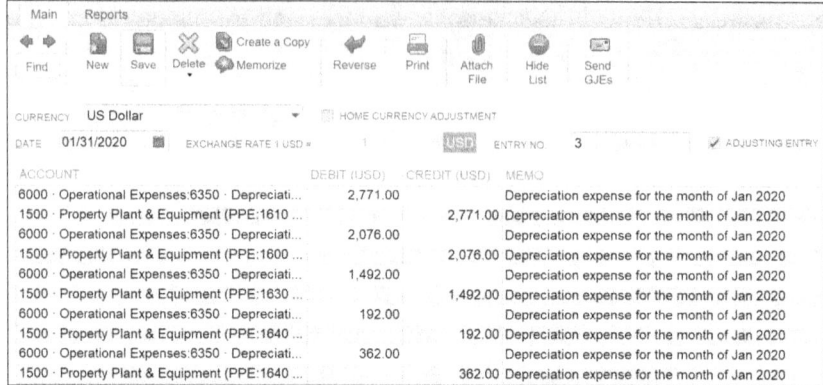

Go to the balance sheet and ensure that the accumulated depreciations deduct the value of fixed asset by the exact amount of monthly depreciation expenses and show the net value of total fixed assets. Verify that the same amount is added under depreciation expense in the Profit and Loss report.

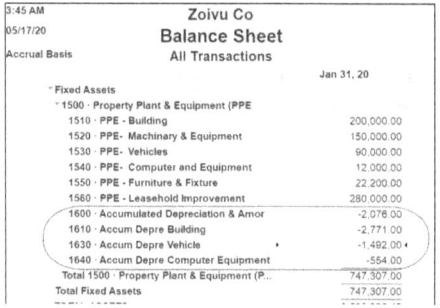

QuickBooks Case Study
Real-World Example (QB)

2. On Jan. 30, the company charged a late fee on the payment to the customer "Walmart Store" for a $ 50 late fee.

Step One: In order to collect a late fee or penalty for any reason, assess financial charges in QuickBooks that can be applied on the customer account. You need to setup the following items:

- **Annual interest rate (%) or minimum finance charges/fixed amount** ($50) based on home currency

- Grace period (in days). For example: If you type 30 in the Grace Period (Days) text box, QuickBooks doesn't start assessing finance charges until 30 days after the invoice is past due.

- Setup the finance charge account (you can add any other income account to be tracked)

- Add other customizations as needed.

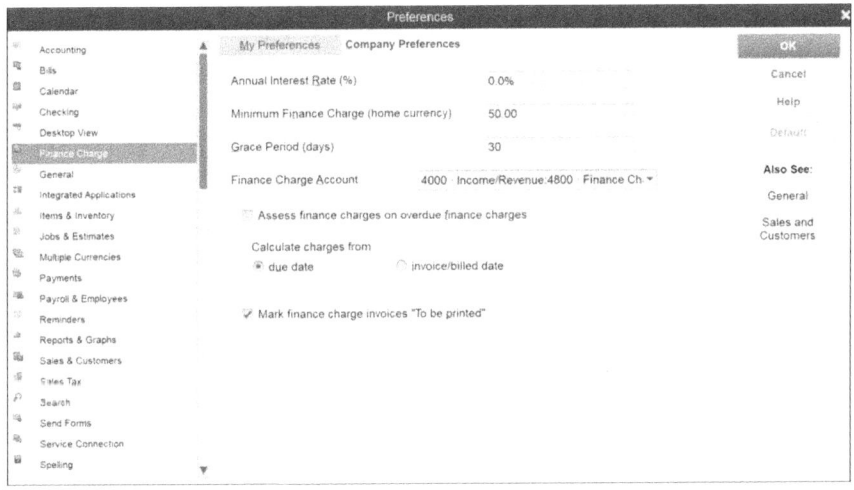

QuickBooks Case Study

Real-World Example (QB)

Step Two: This is the time to assess finance charge on specific customers due to late payment or any financial violation according to your situation.

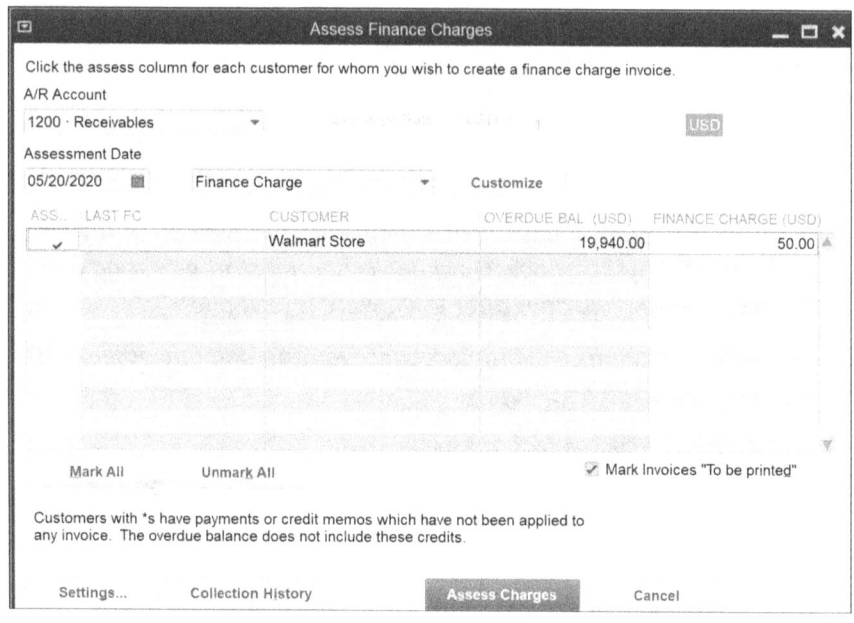

Step Three: What happens next?

Now is the time to go from the homepage under the customer account to the automatic invoice created for the $50 finance charges/late fee. It shows as a collectable (AR) from the customer and the revenue generated shows up under profit and loss account (even though it has not been received yet). This is due to the fact that we set it up as an accrual basis of accounting in the beginning.

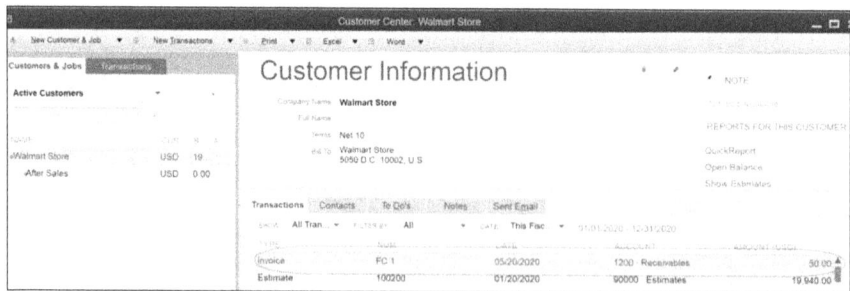

QuickBooks Case Study
Real-World Example (QB)

1. On Jan. 31, the Finance team decided to close the month of January 31st. Prior to that, they made sure to review the closing checklist to prevent missing any adjustments or account reconciliation (sample of checklist is provided in Appendix (B).

Step one closing date:

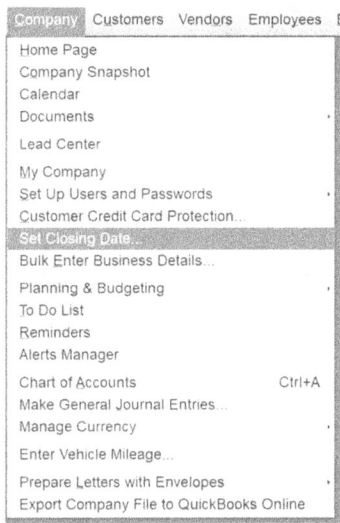

Step two closing date:

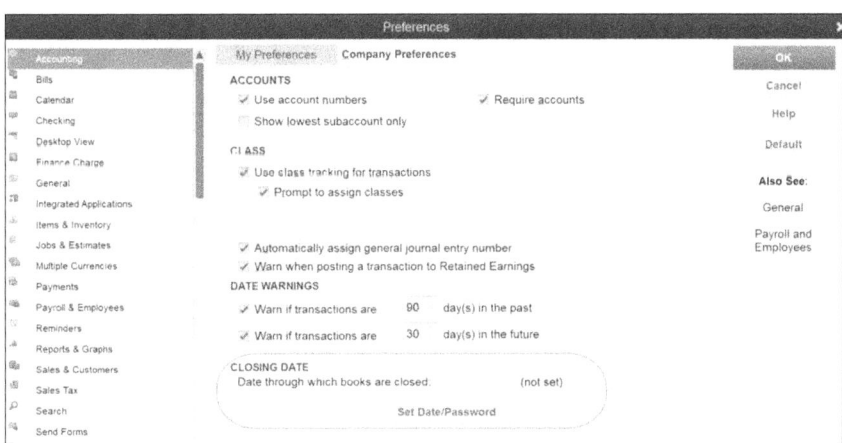

QuickBooks Case Study

Real-World Example (QB)

Set Closing Date and Password

To keep your financial data secure, QuickBooks recommends assigning all other users their own username and password, in Company > Set Up Users.

DATE
QuickBooks will display a warning, or require a password, when saving a transaction dated on or before the closing date. More details...

☐ Exclude estimates, sales orders and purchase orders from closing date restrictions

Closing Date 05/31/2020

PASSWORD
QuickBooks strongly recommends setting a password to protect transactions dated on or before the closing date.

Closing Date Password •••
Confirm Password •••

To see changes made on or before the closing date, view the Closing Date Exception Report in Reports > Accountant & Taxes.

[OK]   Cancel

2. On Jan. 31, the finance department decided to do the bank reconciliation and filed it as a supporting document, including any necessary adjustments made.

As you learned, just like balancing your checkbook and cashbook, you still need to review and make sure your QuickBooks accounts match your real-life bank and credit card statements that you receive at the end of every single month/financial period.

To do the "Bank Reconciliation," the following steps to be considered:

- Make a backup of your QuickBooks file.
- Review your opening balance.
- Prepare for the reconciliation by entering all pending transactions.
- Start your reconciliation and have your bank statement on hand.
- From homepage, go to → "Banking" and then → "Reconcile."
- Select the account or credit card account you want to reconcile.
- QuickBooks will assist you in entering the beginning balance automatically for you and ensure that it matches.
- Enter the "Ending Balance" field in QuickBooks as it appears as the ending balance on the bank statement.

QuickBooks Case Study

Real-World Example (QB)

- If you haven't entered any services, charges, or bank fees/interest fees, you can enter them and assign the account accordingly.
- Review the fields and double-check that everything is correct.
- Select continue to begin reconciling.

For example: We reconciled Zoivu Co. Petty Cash's account (ending in 1020) with no services or bank charges occurred.

Step One For Bank Reconciliation:

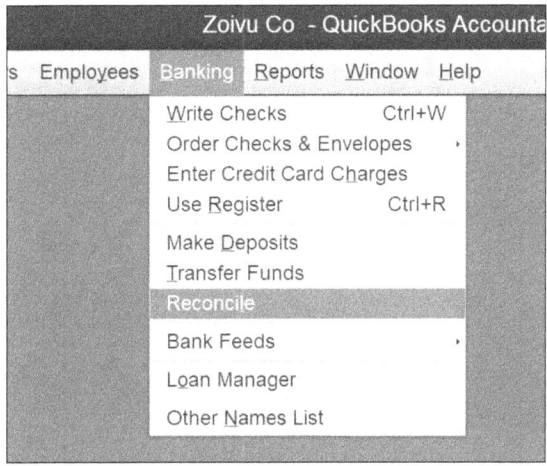

Step Two Bank Reconciliation:

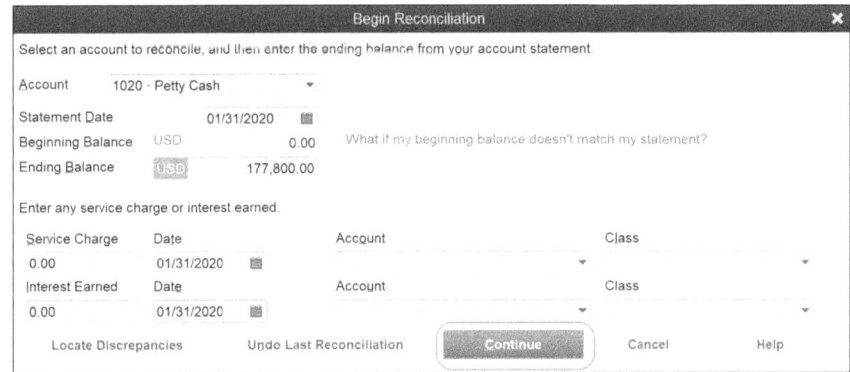

QuickBooks Case Study
Real-World Example (QB)

Step Three Bank Reconciliation:

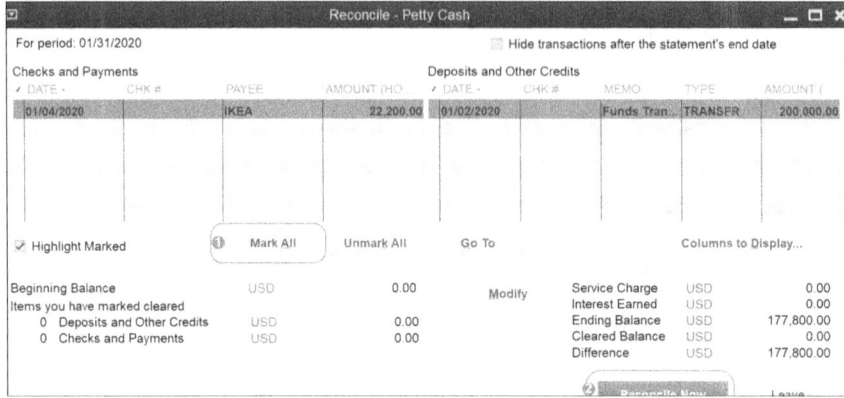

Step Four Bank Reconciliation:

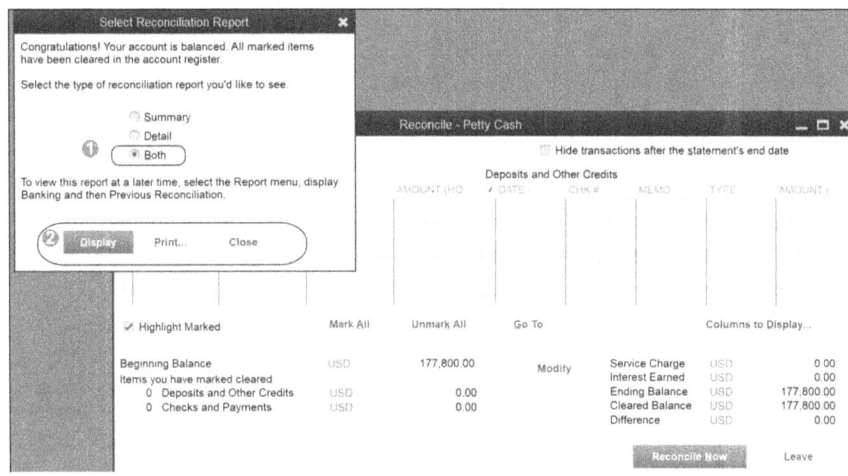

QuickBooks Case Study
Real-World Example (QB)

Step Five Bank Reconciliation:

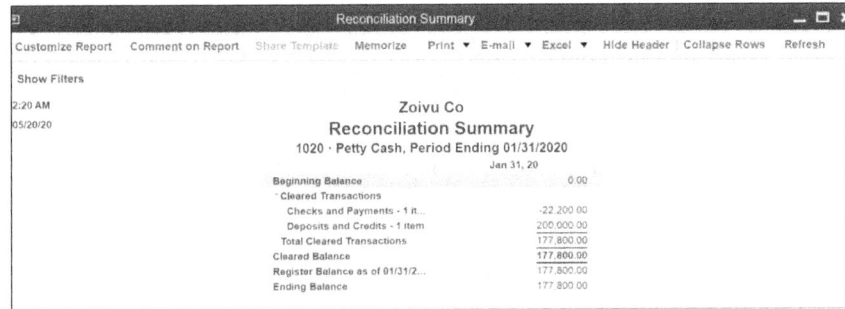

Step Six Bank Reconciliation:

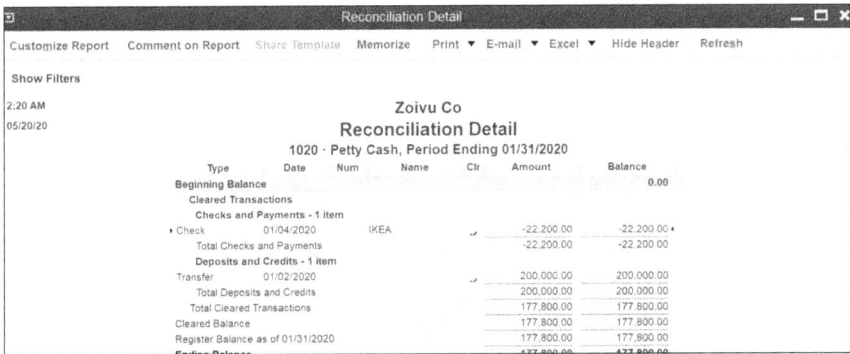

3. On Jan. 31, the board of directors and senior managers asked for the financial statement reports.

You should remember that the following are included in the financial report:

- *Income Statement (Profit &Loss)*
- *Balance Sheet*
- *Statement of Cash flow*

QuickBooks Case Study

Real-World Example (QB)

I.   P&L: Find out how your company is doing financially:

3:03 AM
05/20/20
Accrual Basis

Zoivu Co
Profit & Loss
All Transactions

May 20, 20

Income		
4000 · Income/Revenue		
	4010 · Sales of Pen	5,980.00
	4020 · Sales of Notebook	7,980.00
	4030 · Sales Flipchart	5,980.00
	4800 · Finance Charge Income	50.00
Total 4000 · Income/Revenue		19,990.00
Total Income		19,990.00
Cost of Goods Sold		
5000 · Cost of Goods Sold (COGS)		
	5010 · COGS of Pen	580.00
	5020 · COGS of Notebook	443.60
	5030 · COGS of Flipchart	100.00
Total 5000 · Cost of Goods Sold (CO...		1,123.60
Total COGS		1,123.60
Gross Profit		18,866.40
Expense		
6000 · Operational Expenses		
	6010 · Advertising Expense	10,000.00
	6350 · Depreciation Expense	6,893.00
	6750 · Professional Fees	200.00
	7000 · Payroll Taxes	14,253.00
	7250 · Repairs Expense	2,000.00
	7300 · Salaries Expense	31,752.00
	7500 · Utilities Expense	1,800.00
Total 6000 · Operational Expenses		66,898.00
8000 · TN Tax 9%		13,122.00
Total Expense		80,020.00
Net Income		-61,153.60

QuickBooks Case Study

Real-World Example (QB)

II   Balance Sheet

3:06 AM
05/20/20
Accrual Basis

Zoivu Co
Balance Sheet
All Transactions

May 20, 20

ASSETS	
Current Assets	
Checking/Savings	
1010 · Checking BOA	8,368,573.00
1020 · Petty Cash	177,800.00
Total Checking/Savings	8,546,373.00
Accounts Receivable	
1200 · Receivables	19,990.00
Total Accounts Receivable	19,990.00
Other Current Assets	
12100 · Inventory Asset	120,110.00
1300 · Inventories	24,566.40
1400 · Preapid Expense	11,700.00
1430 · Deposit	70,000.00
Total Other Current Assets	226,376.40
Total Current Assets	8,792,739.40
Fixed Assets	
1500 · Property Plant & Equipment (P...	747,307.00
Total Fixed Assets	747,307.00
TOTAL ASSETS	**9,540,046.40**
LIABILITIES & EQUITY	
Liabilities	
Current Liabilities	
Accounts Payable	
2100 · Payables	601,200.00
Total Accounts Payable	601,200.00
Total Current Liabilities	601,200.00
Total Liabilities	601,200.00
Equity	
3000 · Owners Equities	9,000,000.00
Net Income	-61,153.60
Total Equity	8,938,846.40
TOTAL LIABILITIES & EQUITY	**9,540,046.40**

QuickBooks Case Study

Real-World Example (QB)

III. Statement of cash flows

```
3:10 AM
05/20/20
```

Zoivu Co
Statement of Cash Flows
All Transactions

May 20, 20

OPERATING ACTIVITIES	
Net Income	-61,153.60
Adjustments to reconcile Net Income	
to net cash provided by operations:	
1200 · Receivables	-19,990.00
12100 · Inventory Asset	-120,110.00
1300 · Inventories:1310 · Work-in-Progress	-13,920.00
1300 · Inventories:1320 · Finished Goods	-10,646.40
1400 · Preapid Expense:1410 · Prepaid Insurance	-1,200.00
1400 · Preapid Expense:1420 · Prepaid Rental	-10,500.00
1430 · Deposit	-70,000.00
2100 · Payables	601,200.00
Net cash provided by Operating Activities	293,680.00
INVESTING ACTIVITIES	
1500 · Property Plant & Equipment (PPE:1510 · PPE - Building	-200,000.00
1500 · Property Plant & Equipment (PPE:1520 · PPE- Machinary & Equipment	-150,000.00
1500 · Property Plant & Equipment (PPE:1530 · PPE- Vehicles	-90,000.00
1500 · Property Plant & Equipment (PPE:1540 · PPE- Computer and Equipment	-12,000.00
1500 · Property Plant & Equipment (PPE:1550 · PPE - Furniture & Fixture	-22,200.00
1500 · Property Plant & Equipment (PPE:1560 · PPE - Leasehold Improvement	-280,000.00
1500 · Property Plant & Equipment (PPE:1600 · Accumulated Depreciation & Amor	2,076.00
1500 · Property Plant & Equipment (PPE:1610 · Accum Depre Building	2,771.00
1500 · Property Plant & Equipment (PPE:1630 · Accum Depre Vehicle	1,492.00
1500 · Property Plant & Equipment (PPE:1640 · Accum Depre Computer Equipment	554.00
Net cash provided by Investing Activities	-747,307.00
FINANCING ACTIVITIES	
3000 · Owners Equities:3100 · Investment from George	3,000,000.00
3000 · Owners Equities:3200 · Investment from Michael	3,000,000.00
3000 · Owners Equities:3300 · Investment Charlies	3,000,000.00
Net cash provided by Financing Activities	9,000,000.00
Net cash increase for period	8,546,373.00
Cash at end of period	8,546,373.00

4. On Jan. 31, the finance department received an email from the procurement department, account payables, and sales department for the summary reports of customers and suppliers. Therefore, the financial analyst generates those reports and submits accordingly.

QuickBooks Case Study

Real-World Example (QB)

Accounts Payable Details:

3:17 AM
05/20/20

Zoivu Co
Vendor Balance Detail
All Transactions

Type	Date	Num	Account	Amount	Balance
BP Group					
Bill	01/12/2020	556...	2100 · Payables	158,922.00	158,922.00
Bill Pmt -Check	01/13/2020		2100 · Payables	-158,922.00	0.00
Total BP Group				0.00	0.00
CNBC TV					
Bill	01/18/2020		2100 · Payables	10,000.00	10,000.00
Bill Pmt -Check	01/18/2020		2100 · Payables	-5,000.00	5,000.00
Total CNBC TV				5,000.00	5,000.00
Department of Business and Commerce					
Bill	01/03/2020	10033	2100 · Payables	200.00	200.00
Total Department of Business and Commerce				200.00	200.00
Earth Concstruction					
Bill	01/04/2020	104...	2100 · Payables	350,000.00	350,000.00
Total Earth Concstruction				350,000.00	350,000.00
GIECO					
Bill	01/10/2020	65432	2100 · Payables	1,200.00	1,200.00
Bill Pmt -Check	01/10/2020		2100 · Payables	-1,200.00	0.00
Total GIECO				0.00	0.00
Microsoft Co					
Bill	01/14/2020	121...	2100 · Payables	12,000.00	12,000.00
Bill Pmt -Check	01/14/2020		2100 · Payables	-6,000.00	6,000.00
Total Microsoft Co				6,000.00	6,000.00
Nashville Electricty Services					
Bill	01/25/2020	008...	2100 · Payables	1,800.00	1,800.00
Bill Pmt -Check	01/30/2020		2100 · Payables	-1,800.00	0.00
Total Nashville Electricty Services				0.00	0.00
Nissan Motor Co					
Bill	01/08/2020	656...	2100 · Payables	90,000.00	90,000.00
Total Nissan Motor Co				90,000.00	90,000.00
USA Machinery					
Bill	01/05/2020	14321	2100 · Payables	150,000.00	150,000.00
Total USA Machinery				150,000.00	150,000.00
TOTAL				**601,200.00**	**601,200.00**

Accounts Receivable Details:

3:22 AM
05/20/20

Zoivu Co
Customer Balance Detail
All Transactions

Type	Date	Num	Account	Class	Amount	Balance
Walmart Store						
Invoice	01/20/2020	400...	1200 · Receivab...	Depart...	19,940.00	19,940.00
Invoice	05/20/2020	FC 1	1200 · Receivab...		50.00	19,990.00
Total Walmart Store					19,990.00	19,990.00
TOTAL					**19,990.00**	**19,990.00**

PART (IV)

Appendices and Forms

REPORTING IN QUICKBOOKS

Appendix A: List of a Standard Chart of Accounts

Appendix (B): Sample of Closing Checklist

FROM THE AUTHOR

SOURCES

Appendix A: List of a Standard Chart of Accounts

Appendix A: List of a Standard Chart of Accounts

Below table shows a complete summary of a very basic, simple and standard chart of account example used at Zoivu Co.

No	Account Types	Account No	Account Details
	Assets	1000	Assets (Current & Non-Current)
1	Bank	1010	Checking BOA (Bank of America)
2	Bank	1020	Petty Cash
3	Accounts receivable	1200	Receivables
4	Accounts receivable	1210	A/REC Trade
5	Accounts receivable	1220	A/REC Trade Notes Receivable
6	Another current asset	1300	Inventories
7	Another current asset	1310	Work-in-Progress
8	Another current asset	1320	Finished Goods
9	Another current asset	1400	Prepaid Exp
10	Another current asset	1410	Prepaid Insurance
11	Another current asset	1420	Prepaid Rental
12	Another current asset	1430	Deposit
13	Fixed asset	1500	Property Plant & Equipment (PPE)
14	Fixed asset	1510	PPE - Building
15	Fixed asset	1520	PPE- Machinery & Equipment
16	Fixed asset	1530	PPE- Vehicles
17	Fixed asset	1540	PPE- Computer and Equipment
18	Fixed asset	1550	PPE - Furniture & Fixture

Appendices and Forms

Appendix

19	Fixed asset	1560	PPE - Leasehold Improvement	
20	Fixed asset	1600	Accumulated Depreciation & Amortization	
21	Fixed asset	1610	Accumulated depreciation Building	
22	Fixed asset	1620	Accumulated Depreciation Machinery & Equipment	
23	Fixed asset	1630	Accumulated Depreciation Vehicle	
24	Fixed asset	1640	Accumulated Depreciation Computer Equipment	
25	Fixed asset	1650	Accumulated Depreciation Furniture & Fixtures	
26	Fixed asset	1660	Accumulated Depreciation Leasehold Improvement	
	Liabilities	**2000**	**Liabilities (Current & Long Term)**	
27	Accounts Payable	2100	Payables	
28	Accounts Payable	2110	A/P Accrued Accounts Payable	
29	Accounts Payable	2120	Accrued - Payroll	
30	Accounts Payable	2130	Accrued - Commissions	
35	Accounts Payable	2140	Withholding Tax Payable	
	Accounts Payable	2150	AP Trade	
36	Long term liability	2700	Long Term Debt	
37	Long term liability	2710	Notes Payable	
38	Long term liability	2720	Mortgages Payable	
39	Long term liability	2730	Installment Notes Payable	
	Owner	**3000**	**Capital or Owner's Equity**	
40	Equity	3100	Investment from George	
41	Equity	3200	Investment from Michael	
42	Equity	3300	Investment Charlies	
43	Equity	3400	Withdrawal of George	
44	Equity	3500	Withdrawal of Michael	
45	Equity	3600	Withdrawal of Charlies	
46	Equity	3900	Retained Earnings	
47	Income	4000	Income/Revenue	
48	Income	4010	Sales of Pen	
49	Income	4020	Sales of Notebook	
50	Income	4030	Sales Flipchart	
51	Income	4040	Sales Training manual	
	Income	4050	Finance workshop tax	
	Income	4060	QuickBooks workshop	
	Income	4070	Business consultation	
52	Income	4800	Finance Charge Income	
53	Income	4700	Other Income	
54	Income	4950	Sales Discounts	
	Cost of goods sold	**5000**	**Cost of Goods Sold (COGS)**	
56	Cost of goods sold	5010	COGS of Pen	
67	Cost of goods sold	5020	COGS of Notebook	
58	Cost of goods sold	5030	COGS of Flipchart	
59	Cost of goods sold	5040	COGS of Training manual	

Appendices and Forms

Appendix

60	Cost of goods sold	5800	Inventory Adjustment
61	Cost of goods sold	5900	Purchase Returns and Allowances
	Expenses	**6000-7000**	**Operational Expenses (Admin)**
62	Expense	6010	Advertising Expense
63	Expense	6050	Amortization Expense
64	Expense	6100	Auto Expense
65	Expense	6150	Bad Debt Expense
66	Expense	6200	Bank Charges
67	Expense	6300	Commission Expense
68	Expense	6350	Depreciation Expense
69	Expense	6600	Gifts Expense
70	Expense	6650	Insurance – General
71	Expense	6700	Interest Expense
72	Expense	6750	Professional Fees
73	Expense	6850	Maintenance Expense
77	Expense	6900	Meals and Entertainment
74	Expense	6950	Office Supplies
75	Expense	7000	Payroll Taxes
76	Expense	7100	Printing
77	Expense	7200	Rent
78	Expense	7250	Repairs Expense
79	Expense	7300	Salaries Expense
80	Expense	7500	Utilities Expense
81	Expense	7900	Gain/Loss on Sale of Assets

Appendices and Forms

Forms

A real looks of Purchase Order (PO)

Zoivu Co
ABC Drive
Nashville, TN 37211

Purchase Order

Date	P.O. No.
1/12/2020	12347

Vendor

BP Group
Raw Circle Drive, Boston 02101 US

Zoivu Co
ABC Drive
Nashville, TN 37211

RECEIVED IN FULL

Item	Description	Qty	U/M	Rate	Amount
Polystyrene		5,000	lb	5.00	25,000.00
Tube and cap		1,000,000	ea	0.01	10,000.00
Brass Tip		1,000,000	en	0.01	10,000.00
Tungsten carbide	Tungsten carbide- a ball point	1,000,000	ea	0.01	10,000.00
Ink		1,000,000	oz	0.01	10,000.00
Wood free paper	Wood free writing paper	1,000,000	ST	0.0098	9,800.00
Printing ink		55,000	l	0.20	11,000.00
Cover sheets		5,000,000	ST	0.002	10,000.00
Stitching wire		1,000,000	m	0.01	10,000.00
Sheet pad		1,000,000	ST	0.01	10,000.00
Glue		500,000	l	0.02	10,000.00
Sticker		2,000,000	ea	0.01	20,000.00
TN Tax 9%	TN Tax 9%	1		13,122.00	13,122.00

Total USD 158,922.00

Appendices and Forms

Forms

Inventory Assembly/Bill of Materials

Inventory Assembly/Bill of Materials 4/27/2020 2:35 AM
Item Name/Number New Product:Pen

Manufacturers Part Num				Taxable		
Is Purchased	No					
Sales Price		12.99	Income Account	Sales of Pen		
Cost		5.04	COGS Account	COGS of Pen		
Total Value		0.00	Asset Account	Inventory Asset		
Qty On Hand	0	Avg. Cost	5.04	On Purch Order	0	On Sales Order	0
Pending Builds	0			Build Point	500.000	
U/M	1,000.000			U/M Set	ea	

Item Name/Num	Description	Type	Cost	Qty	U/M	Total
Pen:Brass Tip		Inv Part	0.01	1	ea	0.01
Pen:Ink		Inv Part	0.01	1	oz	0.01
Pen:Polystyrene	Finance workshop tax	Inv Part	5.00	1	lb	5.00
Pen:Tube and cap		Inv Part	0.01	1	ea	0.01
Pen:Tungsten carbide	Tungsten carbide- a ball point	Inv Part	0.01	1	ea	0.01
	Total Bill of Materials			5	-MIX...	5.04

Appendices and Forms

Forms

A real form of an Estimate (a.k.a. Quotation)

Zoivu Co
ABC Drive
Nashville, TN 37211

Estimate

Date	Estimate #
1/20/2020	100200

Name / Address
Walmart Store
5050 D.C. 10002, U.S.

Project

Description	Qty	U/M	Cost	Total
Pen (I)	2,000	ea	2.99	5,980.00T
Notebook (II)	2,000	ea	3.99	7,980.00T
Flowchart	2,000	ea	2.99	5,980.00T
Out-of-state sale, exempt from sales tax			0.00%	0.00

Thank you for your business.

Total USD 19,940.00

Customer Signature

Appendices and Forms

Forms

A real form of an Invoice

Zoivu Co
ABC Drive
Nashville, TN 37211

Invoice

Date	Invoice #
1/20/2020	400500

Bill To
Walmart Store
5050 D.C. 10002, U.S.

P.O. No.	Terms	Project
400500	Net 10	

Item	Description	Est Amt	Prior Amt	Prior %	Qty	U/M	Rate	Curr %	Total %	Amount
Pen	Pen (I)	5,980.00			2,000	ea	2.99	100.00%	100.00%	5,980.00T
Notebook	Notebook (II)	7,980.00			2,000	ea	3.99	100.00%	100.00%	7,980.00T
Flipchart	Flowchart	5,980.00			2,000	ea	2.99	100.00%	100.00%	5,980.00T

Thank you for your business.

Subtotal	USD 19,940.00
Sales Tax (0.0%)	USD 0.00
Total	USD 19,940.00
Payments/Credits	USD 0.00
Balance Due	USD 19,940.00

Appendices and Forms

Forms

Envelope: a form of a birthday card

Zoivu Co
ABC Drive
Nashville, TN 37211

May 19, 2020

Charie M

Dear Charie,

Happy Birthday! Please accept my best wishes for today and the coming year.

I also want to take this opportunity to thank you for being such a valued member of the team. We appreciate your efforts.

Congratulations again,

John
Production

Appendices and Forms

Forms

A real form of a Sales Order (SO)

Sales Order

Zoivu Co
ABC Drive
Nashville, TN 37211

Date	S.O. No.
1/18/2020	1

Name / Address
Walmart Store
5050 D.C. 10002, U.S.

Ship To

P.O. No.	Project

Item	Description	Ordered	U/M	Rate	Amount
Pen	Pen (I)	2,000	ea	2.99	5,980.00T
Notebook	Notebook (II)	2,000	ea	3.99	7,980.00T
Flipchart	Flowchart	2,000	ea	2.99	5,980.00T
	Out-of-state sale, exempt from sales tax			0.00%	0.00

Thank you for your business.

Total USD 19,940.00

Appendices and Forms

Forms

A real look of a Bank Reconciliation Summary

```
2:26 AM                          Zoivu Co
05/20/20                   Reconciliation Summary
                   1020 · Petty Cash, Period Ending 01/31/2020

                                                     Jan 31, 20
              Beginning Balance                                        0.00
                 Cleared Transactions
                    Checks and Payments - 1 item        -22,200.00
                    Deposits and Credits - 1 item       200,000.00

                 Total Cleared Transactions            177,800.00

              Cleared Balance                                     177,800.00

              Register Balance as of 01/31/2020                   177,800.00

              Ending Balance                                      177,800.00
```

```
2:28 AM                          Zoivu Co
05/20/20                   Reconciliation Detail
                   1020 · Petty Cash, Period Ending 01/31/2020
```

Type	Date	Num	Name	Clr	Amount	Balance
Beginning Balance						0.00
Cleared Transactions						
Checks and Payments - 1 item						
Check	01/04/2020		IKEA	X	-22,200.00	-22,200.00
Total Checks and Payments					-22,200.00	-22,200.00
Deposits and Credits - 1 item						
Transfer	01/02/2020			X	200,000.00	200,000.00
Total Deposits and Credits					200,000.00	200,000.00
Total Cleared Transactions					177,800.00	177,800.00
Cleared Balance					177,800.00	177,800.00
Register Balance as of 01/31/2020					177,800.00	177,800.00
Ending Balance					177,800.00	177,800.00

Appendices and Forms

Forms

A real form of a statement

Statement

Zoivu Co
ABC Drive
Nashville, TN 37211

Date: 1/31/2020

To:
Walmart Store
5050 D.C. 10002, U.S.

	Amount Due	Amount Enc.
	USD 19,940.00	

Date	Transaction	Amount	Balance
12/31/2019	Balance forward		0.00
01/20/2020	INV #400500. Due 01/30/2020.	19,940.00	19,940.00
	--- Pen, 2,000 @ USD 2.99 = 5,980.00		
	--- Notebook, 2,000 @ USD 3.99 = 7,980.00		
	--- Flipchart, 2,000 @ USD 2.99 = 5,980.00		
	--- Tax: Out of State @ 0.0% = 0.00		

CURRENT	1-30 DAYS PAST DUE	31-60 DAYS PAST DUE	61-90 DAYS PAST DUE	OVER 90 DAYS PAST DUE	Amount Due
0.00	19,940.00	0.00	0.00	0.00	USD 19,940.00

Appendices and Forms

Forms

A real form of a Credit Memo (CM)

Credit Memo

Zoivu Co
ABC Drive
Nashville, TN 37211

Date	Credit No.
1/20/2020	400501

Customer
Walmart Store
5050 D.C. 10002, U.S.

P.O. No.	Project

Description	Qty	U/M	Rate	Amount
Out-of-state sale, exempt from sales tax	-1	ea	2.99 0.00%	-2.99T 0.00

Total	USD -2.99
Invoices	USD 0.00
Balance Credit	USD -2.99

Appendices and Forms

Forms

A real form of an invoice that containing a logo after customization

ZOIVU	**Invoice**
Zoivu Co	
ABC Drive	
Nashville, TN 37211	

Date	Invoice #
1/20/2020	400501

Bill To
Walmart Store
5050 D.C. 10002, U.S.

Description	Amount
Out-of-state sale, exempt from sales tax	0.00
Total	USD 0.00

Phone #	E-mail	Web Site
615.000.0000	zoivu@co.com	www.zoivu.com

The 20 Key QuickBooks Keyboard Shortcuts

These QuickBooks shortcuts help complete tasks faster and more efficiently.

No	Functions	Keyboard Shortcuts
1	To open help window	Press "F1"
2	To close the current open window	Press "Esc"
3	To see the QB product information or license detail	Press "F2 or Ctrl+1"
4	To open the "find" transaction (such as invoice, bill window)	Press "F3 or Ctrl+2"
5	To increase or decrease the amount	Press " + or –"
6	To go to the next data field	Pres "Tab"
7	To go to the previous data field	Press "Shift + Tab"
8	To copy, paste, undo, and cut	Press "Ctrl, Crtl+V, Ctrl and Ctrl+X"
9	To record or save a transaction	Press "Enter"
10	To delete a selected transaction line	Press "Ctrl +Del"
11	To save and close the current form	Press "Alt +S"
12	To go to your last open forms of the same type	Press "Alt +P"
13	To save and go to the new same forms type	Press "Alt + N"
14	To print a form or list	Press "Ctrl+ P"
15	To memorize a form or transactions	Press "Ctrl + M"
16	To open a memorize transaction list	Press "Ctr +T"
17	To refresh a list or transactions	Press "F5"
18	To create a new invoice	Press "Ctrl +I"
19	To create a new check	Press "Ctrl +W"
20	To close QuickBooks	Press "Alt+A4"

From the Author

Did this book help you?

First of all, thank you for purchasing this book. You could have chosen any other book to read, but you chose mine. For that, I am incredibly grateful.

If you enjoyed this book or found it useful, I'd be grateful if you posted a short review on Amazon. Your support really does make a difference, and I read all the reviews personally, so I can use your feedback to improve this book (as well as for future editions). Feel free directly reach out to me for any other feedback or questions you might have to my email at fraidunmba@gmail.com.

If you'd like to leave a review, please click on the review link on this book's page on Amazon.

Last but not least, I am so grateful to all of those who assisted made this happened including Mr Najibullah Behzad and Dr Oanh Vu for the review, Ms. Debbi Duya for editing and proofreading, the Fiverr experts for formatting and designing of this book.

Thank you again for your support!

Useful Sources

Accounting Tools 2019, Accounting Tools, accessed May 2020, <http://www.accountingtools.com>

Between the Lines (Larry Dignan) 2019, ZDNet, accessed May 2020, <http://www.zdnet.com>

Boundless Finance, Lumen Learning, accessed May 2020, <http://www.courses.lumenlearning.com>

Corporate Finance Institute, Corporate Finance Institute, accessed May 2020, <http://www.corporatefinanceinstitute.com>

International DOI Foundation (IDF) 2016, International DOI Foundation (IDF), accessed May 2020, <http://www.doi.org>

Kieso, D.E., & Kimmel, P.D., & Novak, L., & Trenholm, B., & Warren, V., & Weygandt, J.J. (2015). *Accounting Principles, Volume 1*. Wiley.

Intuit & QuickBooks Inc. Software Company
https://quickbooks.intuit.com/

Madeira, Laura (ACS, Inc.) 2013, Quick-Training, accessed May 2020, <http://www.quick-training.com>

www.ingramcontent.com/pod-product-compliance
Lightning Source LLC
Chambersburg PA
CBHW071357210526
45465CB00001B/140